Curious Minds

SOCIOLOGY & PSYCHOLOGY

A SERIES OF SOCIOLOGICAL & PSYCHOLOGICAL
ESSAYS FOR UNDERGRADUATES

WRITTEN & PRODUCED BY
HELLEN ADOM BA HONS, MA

TAMARE
HOUSE

Curious Minds

by Hellen Adom MA

Published with the services of TamaRe House, UK, 2009

www.tamarehouse.com – info@tamarehouse.com - +44 (0)844 357 2592

Cover by Nexus Design

Printed by Lightning Source, UK, 2009

ISBN: 978-1-906169-65-7

Greetings Reader

Let me first thank you for purchasing this small book which will, hopefully, have a large effect on your wish to understand the subjects covered.

Although you become the subject whilst studying any path in life, we can sometimes feel that a subject being read will take care of itself… A subject studying a subject one hopes will lead to expanded ways of looking at life and living it as best we can.

My aim for this book is to give guidelines to students who are undergraduates in the social/psychology field. I hope my book can be used as a student aid, a form of *rescue remedy*.

Whilst studying as an undergraduate, I prayed for a good read of another's work. However, I also realised that I needed to create my own style and structure in order to access the wealth of information within myself.

I have included in this book the essays which I wrote whilst I was a student that received high, medium, low and failed marks.

My reason for my placing this range of essays in *Curious Minds* is to help you keep focused on what you are trying to explain within your work.

It is so easy to go off on a tangent and place all your dreams, thoughts and wishes into your masterpiece only to find out

later that they are just that… not what the tutor or question actually asked for.

My preambles will also, hopefully, give further guidance as to what the essays can potentially address. The preambles in general look again at the essay content and how I sit with these subjects now, after almost a decade of experience and further studies.

Good tutors, and good advice, make way for a students' growth and direct them on a journey that, in time, will help them to fly. In order to reach our goals we all need confidence and a good starting position.

I hope my insights, experience and vision will help inspire those who think they can't do it! Always remember, we can achieve anything we set our minds on.

As the daughter of a school teacher and nurse, I have lived and learnt that what we see in the physical world has first to be created mentally. The truest saying I know is:

'It's all in the mind'

Good luck and have fun…

Elle (Hellen Adom)

The Essays:

Essay 8:   pg 92

Discuss S. de Beauvoir's argument on the relationship between 'the woman' and 'otherness.'

Essay 9:   pg 106

Final Year Dissertation 1996-97: The View of Autonomy as Spoken by Wheelchair Users in 1997. Historical Theoretical Perspectives.

Preamble to Essay 1: To what extent have public health strategies in Britain in the last 10 years addressed inequalities in health?

The task that we are being asked to perform is to address the question of inequalities in health within the last ten years and to what extent they have been met by the plans that the government has put in place.

My essay looks at the ruling factors which will help direct me to respond to the essay question. Such factors include: which government was in office during the period in question and the extent to which public bodies such as the World Health Organisation (WHO) have egalitarian public health access on their agendas.

I also look at health factors, such as smoking related disorders, which affect particular classes (working) more than they do other sectors of society.

This essay speaks on a range of Primary Care interventions such as hospital care schemes as well as provisions in the public domain such as non smoking publications available through clinics and hospitals.

Eating patterns and social living conditions are also taken into account. The data and statistical information of these better inform researchers and the medical profession, food producers and teachers on best practice.

Essay 1:

To what extent have public health strategies in Britain in the last 10 years addressed inequalities in health?

In order to be able to answer the question we must first look at each part in detail. Firstly, to find out to what extent public health strategies have played their part, we need to find out who and what area of health strategies we are looking at. Also which area in Britain are we talking about? If we look at Britain as a whole, one could be led to believe that the distribution of wealth and money spent on health is equal in all sectors, but there has been a wealth of documentation to show that this assumption is not correct and that there is a North/South divide."

Although there are very affluent areas in Scotland and the North, there is also the greatest concentration of material deprivation." (Whitehead 1992 pg 251). Mortality rates which are used to record the rate of death in a given area can be combined with class and information received and can be made into statistics that record the Standard Mortality Rate or SMR for that area or class." Over the fifteen years, although there was a general decline in death rates, the occupational class differences persisted for stillbirths and deaths. For example, the perinatal death rate of classes IV and V fluctuated at around 150 per cent of the rate for classes I and II for the whole period" (Whitehead 1992).pg267.

Secondly, we must bear in mind that the country has been ruled by a Conservative government over the past 16 years, and this party are mainly those in the upper classes, (as according to the Registrar General's categories which will be looked at later on) people who believe in individualism. As the government is in charge of the health policies their prevailing ideology is used.

Social class and wealth, poor housing and amenities, people's habits and also reasons why people have bad health will be addressed. Inequalities in health have been correlated with income or occupational status in the way that the income gained from job status determines how we are able to live our lives. "Individuals from higher socio-economic positions are on average healthier, taller and stronger, and live longer, than those lower down the social scale" (Giddens 1993 Sociology pg 606).

In this essay we shall be discussing the above comments and trying to find out what barriers there are for people not gaining equal treatments, also the health promotional policies introduced over the past 10 years which are based on the recommendations by the European Community Co-operatives, who are part of the (WHO) and as Britain is part of this union their policies on health stem from here.

Many other areas than those mentioned can affect our health, such as environmental factors, global warming, caused by a hole in the ozone layer which protected the earth from the ultra violet rays surrounding it, this action appears to be causing skin cancers in human beings. Over the years there has also been the rise in poor air quality due to the vast pollution expelled from car exhaust fumes, and industrial waste etc., radio-active leakage's, the list is endless, but due to the size of the essay all these contributors will not be detailed. If we look at some of the WHO's health recommendations (only five of the thirty eight will be listed): 1) The central focus of health promotion is access to health. This means eliminating inequalities in health and ensuring equal opportunities to improve health. 2) The improvement of health depends on an environment conducive to health, especially at work and in the home. 3) Health promotion involves the strengthening of social networks and supports. This is based on the recognition of the importance of social relationships as significant resources in health. 4) The promotion of life-styles conducive to health means developing positive health behaviours and effective coping strategies. 5) Since information and education are prerequisites for informed choices, health promotion should aim to increase knowledge and disseminate information related to health. (Source: G. Scrambler, 1991).

Campaigns used for the WHO's "Health for All by the year 2000" include "Back to Sleep" which sent the message to new mothers to lay their babies on their back whilst sleeping. This campaign was headed by celebrity Ann Diamond who lost one of her children to a cot death syndrome. Media coverage informs the nation usually with the same coverage so if we relate back to the high discrepancies between SEP and mortality rate used earlier we can see that even if information on how to stop a process is given there must be other factors keeping open the wide gap of inequalities open.

"National no smoking day" has also been a recent addition for health promotion and tries to give the public information on how to decrease heart disease and cancers.

"The two major smoking-related diseases, coronary heart disease and lung cancer, were related both to smoking and employment grade. Of the top grade 29 percent were smokers, compared with 61 per cent of the lowest grade."(Whitehead 1992, pg 324 Black Report) this also shows that people in different classes have different behaviour patterns. These factors will be observed later.

As we need to look at occupations, the Registrar Generals scale for occupations is as follows Higher Professional and Managerial positions as class one and Lower professional and administrative jobs in class two, both these classes are seen as the service class. Three, Four and Five consist of Routine white collar, Petite-bourgeois, Technical and supervisory respectively and they are the Intermediate classes. The working classes are Six and Seven, this section is made up of Skilled manual and Semi and Unskilled manual workers.

In the past and present there have been problems in collecting reliable statistical data, as occupational class is mainly used to categorise people, it does not take into account those who are homeless or unable to work due to disability etc. Vera Carstairs points this out in her study on Deprivation and Health in Scotland, she states "not all individuals can be allocated to a social class either in the census population base or in respect of the mortality events which provide the most usual basis for analysis" Also when people are admitted to hospital, "admissions do not succeed in the collection of occupation information which provides the basis for social class." (V.Carstairs 1990). Carstairs also notes that 41% of the population has no car, this can make access to requirements harder. There has also been some differences among sociologists as to what" health" is and what it means. The WHO,1946 described health as "a complete state of physical, mental and social well-being" (Kelly & Charlton 1995 ed. Bunton, et al.)

This seems to be a very unlikely state of being for virtually most of the population. With health being identified in accordance with a person's socio-economic position SEP, there have however been discrepancies in the past, although only minor, that do not support the claim that bad health only affects the less wealthy and as people from the higher SEP were found to have higher incidences of coronary heart disease and higher blood cholesterol according to the Whitehall study (date not known), how can this be if your SEP supposedly guarantees better than average health? An explanation for this can be seen in the salutogenic theory devised by Charlton and White. This theory states that health is something that is "built up from a baseline of susceptibility to disease or death" (Charlton and White, 1995). So because human beings are made up of the same biological material i.e., heart, lungs kidneys etc. we can therefore all fall foul to sickness, but it is the way in which we maintain (or can afford) our status that makes the difference, just because we have more financial access does not mean we necessarily spend it wisely.

Improvements to peoples' health have been mainly managed through educational material and advertisement, but how far have we reached the level that the World Health Organisations policies have specified? The National Health Service (NHS) provides free healthcare in Britain today and has seen major reorganisations since its existence began in 1948. The government fund the service approx. 99% and the rest is made up from donations and sponsorships, but, as with everything else in Britain, cutbacks were needed to try and help the country's economic growth, though quality and efficiency had to be maintained in the health service.

Over the years cutbacks have been seen in areas of hospital and ward closures, this was to implement better efficiency and competition between hospitals and Drs alike. "GPs had long controlled hospital referral; now they would buy in the hospital care for their patients , choosing between hospitals to get the best deal they could....and they would, for the first time, get a budget" (Strong/Robinson 1990 pg 185 the NHS). Specialist areas are something that many hospitals are trying to provide as the best GPs will be rewarded as more patients will be attracted and the more patients seen the more money obtained and the more efficiently the service can be run. However, as time has gone by, technology has improved and expensive new treatments are now a lot more in demand and as "Expanding medical technology has opened up new areas of work, including heart surgery, kidney transplants and hip replacements, which simply were not feasible at the inception of the NHS" (Ham 1985). If we compare this statement for example with figures from the money allocated to the London Borough of Bromley for 1995/96, we can see how improvements in new areas have not been taken into consideration by the government.

Bromley received a total of £170 million, this averages approximately £580 per person yet a hip replacement operation costs £4,059 so this takes up approx. seven people's healthcare allocation and if this operation is needed by many people treatments in other areas will no doubt be affected. Now that peoples' rights to health are being addressed, the patients charter which was introduced in 1990's portrays the patient's rights on how long anyone should wait for an operation or course of treatment in any given area, this action was taken by the government as newspapers and politicians alike were putting pressure on them after a series of patients were found to be dying in hospital corridors and in their homes whilst waiting for an available bed. However, what we need to ask ourselves is, how many people would go and obtain a copy of the charter to find out about their rights to treatment? There was, however, a specification in the GPs new contract on approaches to healthcare "to develop information leaflets and practice brochures which outlined the services they would provide to their patients" (Bunton 1995). But as evidence from many sources suggests, the working class are not as well educated as the upper classes, mounds of written promotional explanations may be of no use to them, and their right to obtain specific healthcare may pass them by.

Primary care or preventative concerns for public health have been shown in the forms of advertisement and trying to educate the nation to look after themselves' better. Health promotion clinics were also introduced so GPs could offer a wide range of services on site, advertisements for margarines that taste like butter but contain less fat, muesli and bran flakes shown to be the breakfast to be eaten, diets of fresh fruit and vegetables, fresh juices to be drunk and decaffeinated coffee all exist, but has any policy maker or health promoter stopped to consider how much such a diet would cost? Many quality foods are more expensive: white bread costs up to 30 pence less than brown bread.

"In 1990 poor households spent 56 per cent of income on necessities (food, fuel, housing), whereas rich households spent 35 per cent of their income on these products." (Whitehead 1992). This clearly shows how the distribution of wealth affects people, anyone on a low income may probably be doing what they can to promote better health for themselves and their families (as even the poor are eating more brown bread according to Whitehead) but worrying about how they will survive , as government benefits have not been significantly increased in past years. Such factors would probably outweigh healthy habits, but unhealthy habits such as smoking are seen more in the lower SE groups as previously mentioned. Causes for this could be having low self esteem because of unemployment or living in bad conditions etc. and as smoking is commonly viewed as a relaxant, the habit may have been formed from this. "Eighty per cent of smokers regret taking up the habit and intend to quit some day."(Dr Trisha Greenhalgh,1994) so many people are aware that smoking is bad for them but giving up a habit or changing a way of life is difficult to do. "Thus smoking and also tranquillisers, are used as a means of coping with pressures." (Calnan & Williams, 1991).

In conclusion, it appears that public health strategies are not taking into account the fact that peoples' whole lives i.e., SE factors, reasons for unhealthy habits and poor housing need to be addressed also. If we now consider the WHO's policy of the central focus of health promotion is access to health. Now that many small or non-central hospitals are being closed or moved to larger hospitals how accessible are these provisions?

As we noted earlier, the lower SE groups have less access to cars and therefore need other ways of getting to appointments etc. Although public transport has put more buses on the road and expanded routes the system is still unreliable and expensive. A study done by Graham in 1979 says, "women going to the hospital antenatal clinic spent twice as long travelling and waiting than mothers going to local GP clinics."(Whitehead 1992). Graham says women would rather spend their time and money doing other things such as catering for their child's needs, and even though this study was done more than 10 years ago accessibility should be of even greater concern now. Alternative strategies need to be enforced such as the opening up or expanding of more adequately run local Drs surgeries, more clinics that are run from there would save people time and money. Prices for "healthy foods" should be reduced to attract the people who may need it most. The Chief Medical Officer for England emphasised that, "despite the continuing general decline in mortality and improvement in health, the forty years since the introduction of the NHS have seen little progress in the reduction of health inequalities... for some variables the differences have grown."(Acheson, 1990, Whitehead, 1992

Authors Note

Now that we are in 2009, has much changed for health inequalities?

At present there are still huge amounts of people presenting at hospitals in large numbers with Diabetes, High Blood Pressure, Kidney problems and the like.

An increase in young people developing old peoples' diseases has placed more pressure on the NHS.

Ways forward can include a higher emphasis by government to provide the nation with clinics and hospitals working together to get the nation fit.

Classes on healthy eating and availability of affordable fruits, vegetables will help people to choose healthier options.

Bibliography

Townsend, Peter and Davidson Nick Ed. The Black Report, Whitehead Margaret Ed. The Health Divide, pgs 251, 332, 333,341, New Ed. Revised and Updated, Inequalities in Health, Penguin Books Ltd. London 1992.

Giddens, Anthony: Sociology, Second Edition fully revised and updated, Blackwell Publishers, Oxford,1993 pgs 606

Ham Christopher: Health Policy in Britain, second edition, Macmillan Publishers Ltd. Hampshire. 1985. pg39

Carstairs ,Vera. Depravation and Health in Scotland, Health Bulletin, 1990. pgs

Charlton, B and White, M. Living on the Margin, Public Health, 109; 1995. pgs 235-45.

Calnan, M. and Williams, S. Style of Life and Salience of Health, Sociology of Health and Illness, 13; 1991. pgs162

Scrambler, G. Ed. Sociology as Applied to Medicine. Third Edition. Bailliere Tindall. 1991.

Abercrombie and Warde, Contemporary British Society, Blackwell Publishers, Oxford, 1994.pg 517.

Bunton, R. Ed. The Sociology of Health Promotion. Routledge. London 1995. pgs 26,79

Strong, P. and Robinson, J. The NHS; Under New Management, Open University Press. England. pg185

Greenhalgh, T. Falling down on giving up, Body and Mind. The Times Newspapers Ltd. pg15

Mark awarded; 62%

Preamble to Essay 2: Person perceptions of Groups and Individuals

Person perception can be viewed as, 'how we see others and ourselves.' It is known within social psychology theory that people may act differently when within groups or crowds than how they act as individuals. This essay looks at Hamilton's theory which itself looks at two different kinds of memory: online memory and memory based thought pattern.

A two tailed test was needed to process the information gathered, this influenced the experimental design. A good piece of research or experiment such as this requires the appropriate structure and components. You are taken step by step through the process until the end result and the discussion rounds everything up.

Social Psychology looks at how we as individuals merge with society. We quickly learn as children what is perceived as good or bad behaviour and this influences our subsequent choices and social behaviour.

How we are socially conditioned through the approval of peers, teachers, and the like can have an effect on how we view ourselves and others.. I hope this work will help in some way to achieving your goals.

Essay 2: Person perceptions of Groups and Individuals

Abstract

The following experiment was conducted in order to see if Hamilton's theory of how we processed information was correct. Hamilton says we use on-line processing when being told about an individual as we try to make sense of the information and we use memory-based processing when we are told about various people within a group. A between-subjects design was used. The subjects read 24 sentences (one on each page) and a bell was sounded every eight seconds as an indication to turn the page and ensure each sentence had the same amount of reading time. A red herring task on guessing a correct answer to win money was then performed to take up time, the students were then asked to write down as many of the sentences as they could remember. Half of the group had been told the information was about a group and the other half told it was about an individual. Subjects also received sentences that described one aspect of behaviour, sociability or four behaviour aspects sociable, intellectual, athletic and political. Results showed the individual as more coherent, and rated more sociable in the one aspect area, the group were significantly more athletic and political.

Introduction

To see how people perceive groups and individuals, an experiment was conducted to see whether similarities or differences showed. David Hamilton says we process information in two ways: on-line processing is when we think that all of the information should be connected so people will use this way of thinking if they are being informed about an individual person to try and fit a whole picture together whereas if they are being informed about a group, Hamilton says we use what he terms memory-based processing, if the information people are given is about several individuals or a group we do not expect to find a whole picture or coherence as with an individual. "Perceivers seek to organize information in meaningful ways to a greater extent when they are processing information about persons than about group members." (Hamilton 1992). This does however depend on the groups entitativity.

It is hypothesized that people remember more about an individual than a group as coherence is expected, and more so in the one aspect category than in the four aspect.

Method

Design:
The experiment was performed using a between-subjects design. This was so the experimenter could obtain two sets of data from the one group without the same subjects doing it

twice as they may remember more information second time around. This was a 2 tailed test.

Subjects:
A total of 169 first year psychology students based at Greenwich University, Avery hill site, were used. Aged between 18-40 approx.
Apparatus/Materials:

A tape recorder was present and a bell sound could be heard every 8 seconds. Subjects were also given an envelope which contained a questionnaire, a small pad with a sentence describing behaviour on each page, and a sheet of paper suggesting how to win a cash prize.

Procedure:
The experiment had two conditions: half the subjects were given written instructions that told them they were being given a description of a group and the other half were told that an individual was being described. Also half the subjects were given one aspect of behaviour, sociability and the others four aspects of behaviour: sociable, intelligent, athletic and political. Subjects were told verbally that they should read each sentence carefully and then a bell would sound every 8 seconds as an indication to turn over the small sentence pad page by page. After the last bell sounded subjects were told to fill in the single sheet of paper that enabled you to win a cash prize if you guessed the answer they wanted correctly. There was, however, no correct answer and this task was used to take up time and to see how much the subjects would remember afterwards. Subjects were then told to fill out the

questionnaire which consisted of writing down as many sentences as they had remembered. Subjects were also told to give percentages of how group/individual rated in sociability or if four aspects given percentages were given for each area. The independent variables were whether the subjects target was group or individual and if they received information on one aspect or four (the range) about the target. The dependent variables were measured by how many sentences were recalled correctly and how the target was rated on all of the four aspects and coherence.

Results:

It is hypothesized that people remember more about an individual's activities using on-line processing than a group activities where memory based processing is said to be used. Also that the coherence rating would be higher in the one aspect group than the four aspect group, as only one type of behaviour is described.

Mean for correctly recalled statements:

Ratings	Group	Individual	t-test	1 aspect	t-test	4 aspects
Social ability	5.2	0.94	5.8	5.9	1.97	5.1
Intelligence	4.4	0.20	4.5	4.1	1.40	4.8
Athleticism	4.2	0.85	4.6	3.8	2.55	5.0
Political Activity	4.0	0.00	4.0	2.9	5.93	5.1
Coherence	3.8	2.07	4.9	4.6	0.94	4.1

Results from our experiment on person perception using t-tests showed a higher significant difference of 1.97 at the p<.05 level in the one aspect area of sociability than in the four aspect area. However high significance at the same level showed the four aspect area were seen as more athletic by 2.55 and more political at the p<.001 level by 5.93. Coherence in the individual target was also found to be more by 2.07 at the p<.05 level.

Discussion:

Asch and Anderson have also worked in the area of impression formation for many years, they, like Hamilton, say that when information on an individual target is given to the perceiver, he or she will aim to find a core of the personality and then build around this. "Therefore the information immediately available is used as a basis for making correspondent trait inferences and evaluative judgements about the person's more general dispositional characteristics." (Hamilton 1992). So a form of stereotyping evolves when making judgements. When inconsistencies arise the perceiver will spend time trying to figure out how this part of the personality fits in with the impression they have formed, as unity or coherence is assumed from the onset whereas in a group "perceivers are less troubled by incongruent behaviours.

They therefore make less effort to resolve these inconsistencies." (Hamilton 1992).

These findings can be seen in Hastie's 1984 paradigm study. If we now look at Donald Campbell's work on entitativity (1958), he says that the coherence we would expect to find in an individual could be found in a group depending on how much entitativity or similarity they have and in what cause they have for being a group, i.e., a family may be perceived to have more entitativity than people in a golfing club, as the family live by the same moral and socialization institutions than individual members of the golf club. It appears, therefore, that Hamilton is supported, as more coherence is found in an individual than a group target based on on-line processing.

People in the four aspect areas were viewed as more athletic and had more political activity than those in the one aspect area. Recall of statements however were more for group than individual. This experiment could have questionable ethics as nervousness occurred due to the subjects being timed and guessing percentages could take place and therefore make the experiment invalid.

References:

David Hamilton, British Psychological Society Annual Conference, 1992, England.

Mark awarded 49%

Preamble to Essay 3: 'You can predict behaviour from peoples' attitudes.' Discuss in the light of the last general election result in Britain.

Prediction can be a funny thing. Sometimes things appear to be certain, a sure win or bet, then something comes and disrupts the certainty, the trend.

How does this happen? There is much to be said on this subject. Different methods of forecasting exist and evolve and contributory factors are re-examined and re-evaluated. There is a weighing up of what appears to be facts compared to what actually takes place.

Voting patterns have been of interest to politicians since time immemorial.

In terms of patterns in voting, it would appear that young people become attracted to a young member of parliament whilst the upper classes have generally voted Conservative, and the working classes Labour.

Political representatives are viewed as defending a particular agenda and the front person representing a particular cause.

This essay looks at longitudinal studies from the past which research social cohesion as a factor in formulating decisions of voters.

Essay 3:
"You can predict behaviour from peoples' attitudes." Discuss, in light of the last general election result in Britain.

According to the works of many psychologists attitudes have been known to predict behaviour. The 1992 election results in Britain were portrayed as such a shock to most of the nation (the votees) but was that really so? The media had voices of surprised newsreaders and large newspaper headlines such as, "Where Did Labour Go Wrong" and Conservative favouring papers saying, "We've Won Again."

How had this change of heart or mind from the voters come about? We grow up with belief systems and attached to them are predictions. One such example would be that God really does exist and the Bible prophets predicted that when the end of the world is coming plagues will be set amongst the people. The onset of the medics evaluating the Aids disease sparked much controversy from the churches and the media who brought physicians and analysts in to predict what would happen within the community, i.e., how many people would die over a given period if a cure could not be found. Now that more, and consistently new, information is being found out about Aids and HIV, the predictions for death rate has decreased and the end of the world predictions did not arrive.

The same paradigm could be said to exist when the pre-election polls predicted that the Labour party was sure to win, this Party even held a pre- congratulations celebration before the final votes were counted, that was how positively they viewed their win to be. Had people changed their intended voting pattern at the last minute due to loyalty and wanting to remain faithful partisans, or had they been persuaded by the Conservative party and their "feel good factors" (rise in state benefits) or by a certain politicians' strategies within the party which could produce rewards for the votee. This would be such as the Minister of Health promising a more effective health system than their rivals and so forth. Or are people irrational and only know what they are doing sometimes whilst the rest of the time they conform to social norms so as not to feel the odd one out? "Being required to behave contrary to one's attitude is a common experience in everyday life,"(Secord, Backman and Slavitt, 1976) but why do we do this/ Leon Fesinger's cognitive dissonance theory may have some of the answers and this work, along with Irving Lorge's, will be looked into.

Attitudes have been described as an expression of our internal thoughts so, "one's opinions or attitudes serve as mediators between the inner demands of the person and the outer environment- the material, social and, most immediately, the informational environment of the person" (Smith, Bruner & White 1975). Sabini states in his book Social Psychology that more recent work has shown attitudes to be evaluations, as people's attitudes can change according to the situation or environment that they are involved in. A study done by Theodore Newcomb in the 1930's at Bennington College on how or whether people's attitudes did actually change and if so whether there was a continuous change, "To what degree does it represent what Herbert Kelman called internalization - real attitude change - and to what degree does it involve compliance - merely expressing the "right" attitude in the presence of people who value those attitudes?"(Kelman, 1958, Sabini, 1994). Newcomb therefore decided to look into this area because students attending the college appeared to take on a more liberal viewpoint as their years there progressed, so being in the college community was a factor involved in the attitude change.

Newcomb discovered by this finding that the amount of integration or time one had spent with college peers was a factor aiding attitude /behavioural change, so the more liberal thinking students became student reps. etc. He found that the people who had changed the least on leaving Bennington where those who scored highly in conservatism, and also that these people where very highly conservative on entrance. Longitudinal research was used in this research, so in 1961 Newcomb tracked down 135 of the 147 women that took part in the study over 25 years previously. He did this to see how many women still held the Liberal view associated with Bennington College and how many did not. The questions for the new study could not be taken from the old questionnaire as the amount of social and political change was great, Newcomb decided to compare voting habits of women who attended Bennington to women who had not but were considered to be of a similar background as them.

Results showed that 60% of the women from Bennington voted more liberally than the other women though 30% of them voted in the same way. It therefore appears that the

Bennington pupils were swayed by their attendance at the college. Most of the students attending Bennington at that time came from upper class, white, Conservative backgrounds therefore their traditions, beliefs and socialization formation would normally be reflected in their attitudes and behaviour. "Social circumstances in which the activity of individuals occurs condition their perception of the world in which they live."(Giddens, 1971)

As old habits are hard to break what contributions might have caused this change ? Several theories have arisen as to why this might happen. Festinger termed his theory 'cognitive dissonance' which was developed from Heider's cognitive work. "The term dissonance refers to an inconsistency between two or more elements... the opposite of one element would follow from the other" (Secord, Backman, Slavitt, 1976).

So a person says one thing and does another and in order for the individual to do this they weigh up the difference, (this is called object appraisal) and go for what favours them most even if it is conflicting to how they originally thought of the situation. So a Conservative voter thinking of voting for Labour would comfort their disagreement with themselves by saying that even though they may not fully support this party, most of their policies would be more beneficial to them than if they were to vote for the Conservatives.

"If the environmental fact either defies categorization or is categorized in such a way as to bring harmful consequences to the person, new attitudes may be developed or shifts in categorization may occur,"(Smith, Bruner &White 1975). There has also been investigative work into the field of candidate association vs statement belief, and a study done by Lorge on this phenomena, was to show how irrational people's attitudes can be. Lorge gave participants statements about political issues and each one was said to belong to a particular MP. The participants then had to rate how much they agreed or disagreed with each one. They were then asked to rate how much they respected certain politicians. After this a second experiment was done to see how much the participants agreed or disagreed with statements but this time the same statements were said to have been originated from different MPs, some of whom had been quoted in the first session. "Lorge found that the subjects degree of agreement with the quotations was dependant on who they thought wrote them,"(Sabini, 1994). With this consideration in mind we can see how voters for the general election can be swayed. Margaret Thatcher held on to the view of no more strikes and was adamant not to give in when the miners decided to do so. On the other hand how many people would be inclined to believe Neil Kinnock, who was Labour's representative at the time of the last election and whose party strongly believes in worker's rights and striking for those rights if need be. In conclusion to what has been said, people's attitudes can predict behaviour but many factors as mentioned need to be taken into account especially when peoples welfare's are being decided.

A general election is more than just a black and white situation as it involves trusting politicians with four years of your life and also weighing up the fact of them sticking to their promises.

Authors Note

If we are to remember anything about politics in 2009, it will probably be about the M.P's expenses.

The nation has trusted the people they had voted for to have their best interest at heart. Yet it appears some of the members of parliament had their own agendas on how to spend our hard earned taxes.

It also appears that it is not a criminal offence to rob the public as long as you pay back. This attitude does little for the up and coming adults who will one day take their place in the workforce with the view that sometimes politics is nothing more than politricks.

Hopefully truth and order will be on the political agenda within the near future.

Bibliography

Edited by Brown, Hedy and Stevens Richard, Social Behaviour and Experience, Multiple Perspectives. Section 10 by Smith. B, Bruner J.S, and White R. pgs 365, 367.(1975). Hodder and Stoughton. England.

Giddens, A,: Capitalism and Modern Social Theory, an analysis of Marx, Durkheim and Max Weber. Pg 57 (1971) Cambridge University press. London.

Secord, Paul, Backman, Carl, Slavitt , David: Understanding Social Life, An Introduction to Social Psychology. Pgs 365,36.(1976). McGraw-Hill Book Company. London

Sabini John, Social Psychology, Chapter 16 & pgs 618,622. (1992). W.W. Norton and Co. Ltd. London

Mark awarded 57%

Preamble to Essay 4: Are hunter-gatherer societies 'environmentally friendly?'

I enjoyed doing this essay. It came at a time in my life when a feeling of liberation within me was starting to grow.
 Having always been inquisitive, it was satisfying, as an adult, to explore this subject with fellow students and researchers interested in how others in our world live. This exploration led me to understand ancient ways of living and the ways of hunting and gathering societies..

However, the ideas I had at the time and the joy in writing the essay took me away from skilful composition and I had to re write it. I failed the first time yet passed the second time around. Getting a disappointingly low mark of 41 (pass mark 40) was not acceptable to me, especially as much work and time had been allocated to the writing of this work.

Researching lives of Eskimos and Inuit tribes opened a whole new world to me in terms of understanding the lifestyles, myths and family structures of other people.

Being able to tell stories of migration when living on the land and knowing which foods are in season creates patterns of hunting and gathering which differ from our own.

Using animals as livestock and clothing material in the particular ways examined shows mankind's ability to adapt to extreme conditions in a range of different environments.

Check the title and see how it matches or does not match with what has been written. When you read this essay carefully, you will realise that although I have filled the tutor with information on the different tribes, I did not point out environmentally friendly ways or compare these ways with an alternative society.

I learned a lot from investigating the material for and then writing this essay. I learned that it is important to keep on track by reading the title accurately, in order to ensure that the question is well addressed.

Always check that you are keeping in line with the title. It is acceptable to demonstrate your passion, as it is a part of you that keeps you motivated whilst producing a piece of work.

Essay 4:
Are hunter-gatherer societies 'environmentally friendly?'

The first impression received by this question is for comparisons to be made, environmentally friendly as compared to whom? Western society or between different hunting and gathering bands such as the !Kung, Nestlik Eskimos, Kalahari Bushmen etc.. If direction was towards western societies then the answer would be of course they are, due to their being a non-industrial, non- agricultural minority population in the world who live off the land and are void of smoke belching factories, car exhaust fumes and cfc gases that damage the ozone layer or mass consumers of anything. This does not mean however that damages in other areas such as endangering wildlife species is not apparent. Even if the latter was considered, hunter-gatherers are probably equally as environmentally friendly as each other, or are they? Due to the scale of the essay I shall only be talking of the !Kung, Ihalmiut or Innuit peoples and the Idthen Eldeli Indians lives and the effects their lifestyles have on the earth.

The dobe !kung can be found living between the areas of Namibia and Angola in south west Africa. These people live in bands of approx 30-40 people at a time though there are other bands a few miles away from each other and people frequently change groups. Their diet consists of 70% vegetable and 30% meat, with vegetables being the !Kung's main dietary contributor, their knowledge of them is great as Lee identifies, "

The !Kung are superb botanists and naturalists, with an intimate knowledge of their natural environment. Over 200 species of plants are known and named by them...and of these a surprisingly high proportion is considered by the !Kung to be edible" (Lee 1979).

Division of labour is structured so women are the main gatherers of nuts, seeds, roots and plant foods which they gather close to home and even though men and children do join in with the gathering activity, only men may hunt. This is because the women's safety is accounted for and it would be easier for family life to continue if the man was injured rather than the woman. Unlike in the western world, the !Kung women's work is not seen as degrading or demoralising but as an equal contribution towards maintaining their lifestyle.

The woman stays close to the home to care for and watch her own and others' children. Also a child in this society can be breast-fed until the age of up to four years old,(breastfeeding acts as a contraceptive) with milk supplements not readily at hand, it makes sense. Societies like this depend upon each other greatly and food is shared equally to enable everyone's survival, so generosity is a main part of their culture, as Meggary states, "They give things away, they admire generosity, they expect hospitality, they punish thrift as selfishness" (Megarry 1995 pg 85).

If someone is selfish name calling and shaming the person usually solves the problem. Pig-headedness or boastful behaviour is also not tolerated as this could cause problems amongst the group. Survival at times can be hard enough without squabbles arising, ostracism is something no-one in the group looks for as being a lone hunter-gatherer would not be possible over a long period of time due to the need for kinship and communal help.

The tools used by the hunters for killing animals consist of bow and arrow, club and the iron tipped spear also included are "sinew for bowstrings and binding, twine of vegetable fibres(for snares), iron fencing wire(for arrowheads), poisonous grubs for arrow poison" (Lee 1979 pg 129). Sharpened arrows can be made by anyone in the band and if that particular arrow kills an animal this is said to be the property of the arrow-maker, who does not keep the whole kill but has the privilege of saying how the meat is going to be used i.e., dried, roasted etc.

The hunter has a tracking skill by which they can tell what kind of animal is around, what sex it is and whether it is injured or not. Killing and catching the animal however is a different matter, the poisoned arrow can take up to a day to work so men will go looking the next day. If the animal was only injured by the shot it could wander for miles before dying and Lee says rather than the men come back empty handed they gather vegetable foods on their route back to bring home.

Work such as household chores and travelling take up approximately two and a half days per week and the rest is leisure time in which the !Kung woman "spends the rest of her time resting in camp, doing embroidery, visiting other camps, or entertaining visitors from other camps. "Whilst... "visiting entertaining and especially dancing are the primary activities of men" (Megarry 1995 pg119). However, dancing is also an evening pastime along with story telling around the fires which sometimes burn all night."

> *The !Kung cooking fire is also a sleeping fire...The woman collect the smaller branches as fuel for cooking, while the men look for the heavy deadfalls, 2 to 4 meters long and weighing up to 30kg for the sleeping fire" (Lee 1979 pg154). Bush-fires are sometimes caused by the heat or on purpose to encourage growth.*

If the !Kungs settle in one place for a few months the ash build up can be plentiful.

Given that the earth does not need a great deal of ash this act could be said to be not very "green." This way of living seems tranquil, settling in one place until food and water supplies are insufficient then being able to move on with all your worldly goods. The weather is warm, although the heavy rainfalls are between October and May, the rest of the year is dry. Sickness and hardships are felt but these conditions are very different compared to those of the Ihalmiut people or inland Eskimos the Innuit.

"(Innuit is the people's own name for their race. Translated it simply means Mankind... Eskimo is not used by them but is a tag applied by the Indians, meaning Eaters of Raw Meat)" (Mowat 1989 pg52).

They live in the Northern Territories of Canada in a very harsh environment where temperatures can plummet to sub zero even -40 degrees in winter time with snow blizzards that last for days. They can also have day-time heat of up to 100 degrees in summer. These people have survived on very little food for many years until an SOS signal was sent by a trader from a tiny trading post near Deer Lake to a place called Churchill, a large trading post that is close to Hudson Bay. The geographic explanations are not excellent as pin-pointing areas where camps or igloos are is difficult to explain, except for North and South. This essay is concerned with events and happenings and not where they happened. Deer Lake trading post is the first point of contact with people from the barren land. The coastal hunter-gatherer Eskimos, however, have a different lifestyle.

"Ihalmiut - which means The Other People- as distinct from those Eskimos who live at the coasts and possess a sea culture" (Mowat 1989 pg53). The Innuit live on an all meat diet so fat is a necessity also because vegetation is hard to grow in such a place, they eat most of their meat raw as willow twig used for fire lighting is very scarce. Survival is the main task of the Innuit and they travel from place to place in pursuit of the Caribou Deer which is their main dietary intake along with ptarmigan, the arctic partridge, the arctic hare and the occasional fish eaten. The deer migrate twice a year, in the early summer the does pass through with swollen stomachs and head south to the flat plains which are their birthing grounds, the bucks follow a few weeks later and after birthing all the deer move south for an unknown reason.

Mowat says it could be that such a large herd will diminish food so quickly that new pastures need to be found or, "mosquitoes and black flies abound so richly in the Barrens, that for weeks on end a wise man does not stir from his dark cabin by day" (Mowat 1989). The autumn also brings the Caribou through certain regions and the Innuit people capture enough to last until the next migration, with the climate being on their side, they can store meat in icy reserves for months.

> *"During the fall hunt the Ihalmiut must collect sufficient fat to meet the year's needs, but there is never enough to provide fuel, food, and heat together" (Mowat 1989). These people haven't always lived like this for all their years of existence but around the 1920's they came across white men who had come in search of white fox pelts to ship abroad as the fur industry was booming.*

With the Eskimos being people who lived amongst these animals and cold conditions they were the perfect option to do the white man's work for him and in return for the pelts they were given guns, beads and flour.

This trading went on for many decades, however, whilst the men, the hunters became so preoccupied with hunting foxes, their food supplies diminished slowly and their reliance upon the white man for his rewards became dependence until one day when the hunters took their catch to the trading posts only to find no-one there. The hunters returned year after year to a closed trading post, the white men had disappeared due to the slump in fur prices on the world market. The Eskimos had not only lost track of the deer but also their fine tool making skills."

The Ihalmiut had forgotten how to make cunning bows of horn, during the long years when they had no need of bows" (Mowat 1989 pg 56). Consequently many of the people starved before help from the Canadian government arrived.

In another area of the Barranlands lived inhabitants called the Idthen Eldeli Indians which means Eaters of Deer. There were known to be approx. 2,000 of these people left in 1900. They too came into contact with the white traders around 1930 and were asked to bring extortionate amounts of deer tongue to the trading hut in exchange for guns and ammunition.

The Indians could not possibly eat all the meat of 50,000 yearly slaughtered deer so their bodies were left to rot in the lakes and rivers. Deer numbers swindled so much that now only one migration passage is used meanwhile the Ihalmit wait and those who cannot wait die. Many Eldeli Indians died of starvation as they had not realised due to their caring ways that by looking after the white man's interests they badly neglected their own.

The bushfires of the Dobe area can not be seen as unnecessary harm being done to the environment as it allows for fresh vegetation to grow which is much needed for these nomadic peoples lifestyles. Dead wood from trees is used for fires that burn the whole night, as the !Kung are constantly on the move a complete disappearance of its existence would be highly unlikely.

The lives of the Ihalmiut and the Idthen are also environmentally friendly as everything gets used, the fat from the animals has many uses and like the !Kung their tools were made from materials of the land. We must remember that the land has supported how hunter-gatherer bands live for many centuries and even though starvation and disease may have claimed many lives no one lives forever. Based on the information gained the !Kung along with the Ihalmiut and Idthen could be said to be environmentally friendly until the arrival of the white man and his ideology."agents of the government have been sent out to tell the survivors of the Idthen Eldeli that they must learn the arts of "conservation" (Mowat 1989).

Now that many western countries have noticed the damage caused to the planet and its inhabitants with rays of ultra-violet light beaming through the Earth's atmosphere and affecting fair skins with cancer etc., oil tankers and burst pipes causing slicks that kill otters and other wildlife, near extinction of rhinos as the horns are used for aphrodisiacs, mass seal hunts, etc. etc. They are now signing treaties world-wide for animal and plant conservation, after years of using non-recycled or non-recyclable materials, a "greener" way of life must be the way forward.

2009 NOTE:

In this essay, I needed to display how people lived environmentally friendly, yet I mixed my passion for the hunter gathering societies with how the races treated or ill treatment of various groups. Exploitation is what I focused on due to wanting to highlight unfairness.

The world can only be made fair by humans wanting this course of action, and although Fair Trade is on every employer's lips at present, no one has ever talked of compensation for the many years on unfair trade.

Here's to hoping a new time will emerge which includes taking care of each other as if they are our own family.

Bibliography

Mowat Farley, <u>People of the Deer,</u>(1989), Souvenir Press, London.

Megarry Tim, <u>From the Caves to Capital,</u> Readings in Historical and Comparative Sociology, (1995), Greenwich University Press, England.

Lee Borshay, Richard, <u>The !Kung San,</u> Men, Women and Work in a Foraging Society, (1979), Cambridge University Press, London.

Mark Awarded 41%

Preamble to Essay 5: Is Psychiatry fundamentally about Social Control?

It is said that history has a way of repeating itself. Analysing the past can give us greater clarity into how to proceed with the future.

Social control is one way to keep the masses thinking and feeling life is good or worthwhile. The rationale behind this is that otherwise our motivation will disappear and we may turn to express a more destructive self. This would create disastrous results for the individual and the society each inhabits.

Psychiatrists have been accused of creating their own trade from other peoples' misery. Their profession and expertise emerged in the late 18th and early 19th century. I discovered writers such as Foucault and J. H Burke who spoke up for the individual, and their right to be 'well'.

The prison population has grown in recent years. Some say this is due to bad parenting, lack of moral conduct or plain bad mindedness in individuals. Personally, I feel that we need to look carefully at our society and individuals therein, in order to clarify whether psychiatry is about social control or social help.

Psychiatrists have been seen as having peoples' lives literally within their hands, at the stroke of a pen, a person's freedom, livity and culture can be turned on its head.

New forms of living and dealing with a mental condition are being introduced such as Art and Dance therapy. I think more avenues such as these need to be both enhanced and integrated within psychiatry if we are to restore ourselves to the caring society that we purport to be.

Essay 5:
Is Psychiatry fundamentally about Social Control?

In order to be able to answer the above question we first of all need to define what is meant by social control and what psychiatry consists of. Drever, 1952 describes psychiatry as, "A specialized study and practice dealing with mental and nervous disorders; generally employed in a somewhat wide and indefinite sense, inclusive of psychopathology, and even some branches of psychology" (Drever 1952:229). Such branches of psychology are psychotherapy and psychoanalysis, both these methods try to treat the psyche or cognitive element of an individual who has become confused or disorientated with their roles in everyday life.

Durkheim says that society is like a machine and the individuals in society are cogs within the machine making it work for the benefit of all. When a cog breaks down i.e., due to death or mental illness it is easily replaced as there are always unemployed, surplus others. If society is considered as a machine it does not need cogs breaking down, or dis-regulating the system that it is supposed to be supporting. An investigation into why the cog has broken down (except for death & retirement) could be said to be a psychiatrist's job. This essay will look into why an individual can break down and cause friction or dangerous acts between themselves and society. It will also take into account the need for social control within a society. Many answers can be found if we look into the historical concept of how and why psychiatry came about. Social control is something which is needed to keep the individual within a society safe, so rules need to be obeyed, "T. Parsons (1951) defined it as the process by which, through the imposition of sanctions, deviant behaviour is counteracted and social mobility maintained" (Abercrombie et al 1988).

Psychiatry is a division which could be seen as a form of social control as its presence is involved in the country's judicial system, as well as other systems, that deal with sentencing and imprisoning individuals who could be dangerous within society. Deviant acts vary in their degree of seriousness, and anything from a man flashing, a woman shoplifting or someone committing murder is offensive enough in the laws eyes to bring the deviant individual to court and be questioned about their actions, before being sentenced. Hare says,

"Society has many rules, some formalized in laws and others consist of widely accepted beliefs about what is right and wrong. Each protects us as individuals and strengthens society's fabric" (Hare 1993:89).

However, society should not be seen solely as a group of people who do not have any faults, as certain actions are permissible and have no fines. There are people within society that may have abnormal or deviant ways i.e., people who choose to live on the street, people who dress oddly or talk to themselves whilst out in public, this sort of action is not punishable by law and these people are sometimes called "eccentric." As they are not harmful to others or themselves psychiatry pays little or no attention to this area. Eccentricity, however, makes us as humans draw a line between madness and sanity/genius. Words used in everyday speech such as the "mad professor" are indicators as to how the human mind can change its way of thinking due to stresses of daily life or work etc.

The term "diminished responsibility", is used widely nowadays in courtrooms, during media coverage and when detailing news of a specific case, that fascinates or confuses the public. Especially when no visible cause as to why it happened are evident, such as a loving mother kills her baby yet claims she did not know what she was doing at the time. However, if we look back at some of the court cases that happened at the beginning of the 19th Century we can see how such rules came to try and prevent the mentally ill from being wrongly imprisoned due to their actions. "The intervention of psychiatry in the field of law occurred in the beginning of the nineteenth century, in connection with a series of cases whose pattern was about the same, and which took place between 1800 and 1835. A case reported by Metzger: a retired officer who lives a solitary life becomes attached to his landlady's child. One day, "with absolutely no motive, in the absence of any passion, such as anger, pride, or vengeance," he attacks the child and hits him twice with a hammer" (Foucault 19:129). More cases like this are documented by Foucault, such as "Selestat case in Alsace.

During the extremely hard winter of 1817, when famine threatens, a peasant woman takes advantage of her husband being absent at work to kill their little daughter, cuts off her leg and cooks it in the soup." A case from Scotland is also told where, "a certain John Howison enters a house, he kills an old woman whom he hardly knows, leaves without stealing anything and does not go into hiding. Arrested, he denies the fact against all evidence; but although the defence argues that it is the crime of a madman... Howson is executed" (Foucault:129).

All of the above criminals were considered as mad as they had no motive for their actions (except maybe the mother killing her daughter whilst a famine was on and starvation may have played a part). The legal system saw growing numbers of such cases and explanations were needed and "If psychiatry became so important in the nineteenth century, it was not simply because it applied a new medical rationality to mental or behavioural disorders, it was also because it functioned as a sort of public hygiene" (Foucault:134).

The streets and courtrooms needed to investigate mans' dangerous side and look into any connecting factors that may have triggered off such episodes of madness. The mentally ill were therefore cleared off the streets and sometimes out of families and into institutions were they could be kept an eye on and drugged, if need be, to keep the peace. Psychiatry was born, and today this field deals with many normal people who find it hard just to live their daily lives. With psychiatrists having power within the judicial system, sometimes advantages can be taken with patients or people being detained in prison cells.

Johnstone (1989) talks of a 20 year old girl named Jenny whose mother became worried about the strange action of her child locking herself in her bedroom and playing records. When going to the Dr's herself she told him that her mother treated her like a child, the GP concluded that she was depressed. "The next evening, he received a frantic telephone call from Mrs Clark, who said that Jenny was refusing to come down for meals, and she was sure her daughter must be crazy. The GP dismissed this idea, and advised Mrs Clark to leave Jenny's food in the oven" (Johnstone 1989:73). Friction between mother and daughter escalated over the next few days and the duty psychiatrist along with an on call GP came to the house, Jenny shouted at her mother "I hate you! You just want to keep me like a child! You never leave me alone!' while her mother retaliated at the top of her voice 'You're crazy! You're mad! You should be locked away!" (Johnstone:74).

Under the law, in the mental health act (1983), Section 63 states that "consent of a patient shall not be required for any medical treatment given to him for the mental disorder from which he is suffering" (HMSO, 1983:55). This is what happened in Jenny's case. "Forms were signed for compulsory admission. Struggling desperately and shouting that she was sane, Jenny was physically forced into the ambulance. Over the next few days, Jenny slowly lost her hold on reality. Partly due to the side effects of the large dosage of drugs, the bright young woman was transformed into a shuffling creature with slurred speech and vacant eyes" (Johnstone:74/5).

Although Jenny's case is documented briefly, whilst reading it, none of her actions appeared to be describable as mad, she appears to be a young woman wanting to live at home yet wanting to live her own life. Her mother, however, seemed to have a problem of letting go as Jenny was finally released and behaved like a good little girl. Another story of abusive care linked to section 63, is that of Kate,a 20 year old student. She was depressed after being dumped by a man she thought would become her husband. Instead of being hospitalised, "mutual friends brought her to Kingsley Hall, a former community in the East End of London where people with emotional crisis could come for help and to live as an alternative to mental hospital" (Berke, 1979:77). Her parents came to get her one day saying she needed proper treatment.

"Against her will she was taken... put to bed and immediately given a course of electroshock treatments" (Berke:78). Months later a member of Kingsley house saw Kate who looked confused, she had a notebook and was trying to recall names and faces that fitted with addresses of previous friends. "She said she was very well, she had had several courses of ECT, she was living at home. It was getting late and mummy expected her home for tea. What happened to Kate is an example of the exercise of social control in the guise of medical care" (Berke:78)

The above descriptions are few of the many documented. Psychiatrists however defend their stance and Professor Alberto Parrini, a psychiatrist, says that, "It is a commonly held view, and quite wrongly held, that the role of psychiatry is to control people" (Parrini, BBC:27). Parrini talked of a law 180, which is used in his country Italy. "Law 180 is intended to take care of a person who suffers. We must not use medical skills as an instrument of oppression" (Open Mind, BBC:27). I do not know if such a law is issued in Britain, though clauses for patient's safety must be provided.

In conclusion to what has been written, the evidence shows that psychiatry has been brought in as part of the judicial system over a certain period of time. Prevention of dangerous individuals in society was one of the main reasons it was brought in. "Such an interest in the great crimes "without reason" does not - indicate on the part of psychiatry a desire to take over criminality, but a desire to justify its functions: the control of hidden dangers in human behaviour" (Foucault 19:135).

Nowadays, unless preventative laws are made strong enough for the guilty person to argue their point, many normal people will become submissive but abnormal. Psychiatry fundamentally is therefore not about imprisoning individuals, but trying to help out mentally ill people. Even though the horror stories above show no mercy and forceful actions were used to restrain people, it was family members who gave their consent and misdiagnosis of facts by the parents and Drs did not give these young women any choice. At the end of the day the law is the law and this is what stands in the way of decision making.

Bibliography

BBC Education, Madness: A Study Guide Accompanying the BBC2 television series Madness by Johnathan Miller.

Berke J.H (1979) I Haven't Had to Go Mad Here: The psychotics' journey from dependence to autonomy, Pelican Books, England.

Foucault M Politics, Philosophy, Culture - Interviews and Other Writings 1977-1984: Chapter 8.The Dangerous Individual.

Hare R.D (1994) Without Conscience: The Disturbing World of the Psychopaths among us, Warner Books, London.

Johnstone L (1989) Users and Abusers of Psychiatry: A Critical Look at Traditional Psychiatric Practice.

Mark Awarded 70%

Preamble to Essay 6: What are the major arguments for a national food policy in Great Britain?

If ever there was a subject that is continually on our minds, it is food. It's a product none of us can do without.

In 1995, which was around the time of this essay, food, for many, was 'just something we ate'. There were people who, on a diet, kept calorie counts; veganism and vegetarianism were on the uptake, yet the kind of scrutiny food came under, in the public arena was relatively limited, unless there were food health scares.

However, now, in the early twentieth century, we appear to be a little more ahead in terms of food consciousness. Ingredients, calories and the recommended daily allowances are all placed on the wrapper or on the box when we purchase food. It appears to give society the choice to see what they are eating. It produces options enabling clearer choices. It therefore places a part of the responsibility for decision making on what and how to eat on the individual.

Advertisements for 'junk' food still get major media air play, though healthy food ads are becoming almost as frequent.

The frequency of cases of obesity, heart attacks, strokes and strongly nutrition-related disease are weighing heavily on the NHS at present. The need for the public to be more responsible through the use of self will or power has been forced onto the health agenda.

This has resulted in a public campaign to combat the mess made by eating what we like, how we like it and whenever we choose to. Ideas for optimal daily food intakes are now to be found on posters, leaflets and the like. This is to drive the message home that "We are what we eat", in the words of the popular TV food programme.

Essay 6:
What are the major arguments for a national food policy in Great Britain?

In order for an argument to be presented we first need to find out what a national food policy for Great Britain would mean, in the sense of, is it going to be a rigid set of rules defining what people should eat or not eat?

How much leeway is given to the individual on the choice of goods being offered by the policy holders? Points of whether the economy in Britain will be drastically affected by such a change as where fresh fruits and vegetables are not as highly priced as other goods such as refined white sugar or expensive meats. "Fat, sugar and salt are profitable commodities; fresh cereals, vegetables and fruit less so" (Walker & Cannon, 1984).

The livelihood of farmers, agriculturalists and fishermen would be affected as they are the main producers of such goods and the government supports them by buying all their stock, so a method of fairness would need to be established. The issue of food safety would have to be raised as the public appear to have lost faith in what the government and some farmers say is true, as the recent outbreak in Bovine Spongiform Encephalopathy or BSE, as it is more commonly known as, and hear-say that there might be a human equivalent of the disease.

Many other arguments that affect food policies such as surplus food supplies stored in warehouses for years, animal fodder ingredients and questions of meat lenience cannot be argued due to the size of the essay. Also as Great Britain could be said to be multi-cultural and different foods are consumed the individual will be seen as one group, as most of our bodies are made up of the same organs.

When we talk about food and polices' being made surrounding that fact, we need to make a definition of what food is. "To put it in the form of a paradox: food is what we eat, but not everything we eat is food. The explanation for this lies in the fact that food has a function - to keep us alive and healthy - and unless what we eat contributes to this function in some way, it should not strictly count as a food" (Fox & Cameron 1989). Though there are many food acts how many guard the consumers' welfare? Most of the acts are provided for food producers.

With food being something all human beings need to consume and linked with the view that food gives us our health status to a certain degree i.e., if we contract food poisoning or eat something that disagrees with our body functions, sickness or pain usually tells us something is wrong and thus we can avoid or be more sceptical, knowing that we can get damaged by something we eat and therefore be aware of it.

Children should also be counted as part of the nation as they are the next adult generation and if diets are to be changed in favour of better life quality who better to target than the next generation? If we continually think in a manner that pie and chips or fast foods including fizzy drinks have no immediately noticeable consequences, people will think it fine to feed their children in this way. "Why do school children prefer fizzy drinks and crisps to a well balanced school meal?" (Fentem, 1981). So what other concerns sparked off a need for a national policy and how far have we come towards that goal?

Sir Keith Joseph, Secretary of State for Social Services, set up a working party which included people from the Department of Health and Social Security (DHSS); the Health Education Council (which is funded by the DHSS); and the British Nutrition Foundation (which is funded by the food industry). In essence, the main recommendation of the working party stated that, 'there is an urgent need for... simple and accurate information on nutrition.' (Walker and Cannon, 1984).

Health officials and individuals would like to know more about the food we eat. As a result of the working parties concerns, the National Advisory Committee on Nutrition Education (NACNE) was formed in 1979. "Various interests were represented on NACNE. The DHSS and the Ministry of Agriculture Fisheries and Food (MAFF) were powerful members, as were spokesmen for the food industry and the British Nutrition Foundation. The Health Education Council, its Scottish equivalent, and a number of professionals concerned with the theory and practice of health and nutrition, were also members." (Walker and Cannon 1984).

With the British diet consisting of many fast foods, such as MacDonalds, easy cook meals of convenience, which advertisers say save people time and energy, the population as a whole could be said to be unhealthy. "It is well established that too much saturated fat in the diet (as in the typical British diet) is harmful and is a basic cause of heart disease." (Cannon and Walker,1984). The increase of diseases and illnesses such as Coronary Heart Disease (CHD) and stroke shows that diet has an effect on how our bodies can react to food ingredients. Our bodies are like machines with the brain being the motor. As food keeps our body going we need to be concerned about what we eat in order to treat it well.

This wellness includes eating food which our body requires i.e., nutrients in the form of fruit and, vegetables, these are sometimes known as protective foods. We also need energy foods like bread, potatoes and sugar and also food that helps us grow and provide calcium and other nutrients, such as is provided by milk, meat and eggs. The NACNE report says that in order for British people to reach a state of bodily healthiness we need to cut down 50% of our sugar and salt intake, eat less meat and more cereals, oats, fish etc. "Not only was the NACNE report confident in the recommendations it made, it quantified them as well" (Mills, 1992).

Such recommendations' means bad news for many people in the food industry as changes in compositional standards will affect them also. "Changes to food labels would increase their costs and unfavourable information on those products could reduce sales" (Mills 1992). People's jobs could be cut or made non-existent as a result. As mentioned previously outbreaks of diseases such as BSE in cows has been linked by media resources as having a human equivalent. The government are strongly protesting, saying this statement is untrue and that beef is perfectly safe to eat though many health professionals disagree.

Farmers and food stores alike noticed a slump in sales just before Christmas last year as people were unsure about what or whom to believe. Actions like this prove that most people do take an interest in what they eat. "Farmers must broaden their appeal to embrace the interests of consumers and environmentalists if they are to regain the confidence of the public" (TIMES, 1991). At least if the people that make up the nation are shown a choice of what is available for consumption, many would seek the healthiest one.

An example of this can be seen in a product such as Robinsons' dilutable juices, the manufacturers of which revealed that their low sugar juice outsells the original brand by four to one. "The public demand for brown and wholemeal bread and cereal products has been increasing in recent years" (Femten, 1981).

Now that we are in the nineties, the emphasis is on looking after our bodies by taking up a form of exercise and eating healthily. The idea of three square meals a day no longer exists as this concept was used mainly to build up the nation's strength after years of rationing during World War Two. Stronger health warnings on packets of cigarettes

'National No Smoking Day' etc. have all been implemented and given the nation food for thought but, "To focus exclusively on the cognitive aspects of food choices to the exclusion of economic means of intervention is to limit drastically the possibilities of implementing a nutritional policy" (Mayer & Dwyer,1979).

Past evidence gained by many sociologists and researchers, show that people from poor or low income families suffer more from diseases and malfunctioning bodies (which cause early deaths) than those from more affluent backgrounds i.e., homeowners or high income families. With Britain having a North/South divide it is evident that our wealth position or socio-economic position plays a part in how well we are able to look after ourselves. People in the North of England earn less money than their Southern counterparts, and even though the cost of living is in line with their earnings, depravation is rampant."Death rates were highest in Scotland, followed by the North and North-West regions of England, and were lowest in the South-East of England" (Whitehead 1992). All deaths, of course, cannot be linked to food or nutrition but, on a Liverpool housing estate, "One source of infection was traced to unhygienic mobile food vans which residents used because no shops had been provided on the estate" (Whitehead,1992). Surely it is in the governments' interest for them to look after its citizens in a more positive order, as food is seen as a necessity. Proper provisions need to be available for all. Not only does it appear that the government and food industries are overlooking this generation's needs but also those of the future.

If we relate back to the point about children's diets and which foods they prefer, it is clear that the fast foods seem more appealing than a 'staple diet' or one proposed by NACNE. The European Economic Community (EEC) could be said to be hindering better health options. For example, as fruit is part of the balanced diet, there is a need to look after the children's concerns and as Walker and Cannon rightly suggest, barriers in the form of legislations are set up without public consultation: "The EEC discourages diversity by insisting on strict grading standards for size. Tiny apples are rejected. But can a child munch its way through a 6-ounce apple, let alone keep hold of it?" Not only would it be encouraging for the child to eat fruit regularly due to its size and manageability but it could also be a way of introducing a focus on fruit for the next generation. "It's a pity the EEC has classified these apples as sub standard" (Walker & Cannon, 1984).

We need to include more fruits, cereals etc. in our daily lives to help enable or sustain good health then we need to find ways of introducing it in a manner in which the public does not feel forced or unable to change from where they presently are. Views such as eating too much fruit is not good for you, stigmatize certain goods. People should already realise that too much of anything is usually not good for you or your body. "It is a commonly held view in Britain that eating too much fruit will have a catastrophic effect on the bowels. One fruit too many and there will be terrible consequences" (Walker & Cannon, 1984). This statement couldn't be further from the truth, as a body that clears out its waste on a regular basis must be cleaner and work better. As this statement was made over ten years ago many people's attitudes towards fruit are changing in the Nineties, and fruit is seen more in a positive light.

In summary, we can see the major arguments for a national food policy. The public want more information on how to eat healthily and live healthier lifestyles as the NACNE report showed, "The response of local authorities, schools and health authorities to the report demonstrates that these agencies had wanted guidance" (Mills, 1992). Food producers and manufactures need to label their foods with easier to understand codes, as not everyone can translate energy values equivalent to your body weight. Ingredients need to be specified. "For example, in 1980, the Food Standards Committee (FSC) of MAFF recommended that the regulations governing meat products should be tightened because consumers were not aware that water was being added to products" (Mills,1992. Additives and emulsifiers that sometimes add nothing to the food being sold except weight; need to be cut out if they not needed for food preservation, etc.

"The fact is that every component of the food system can be acted upon to bring about improvements of the nutritional status of large numbers of people." (Mayer & Dwyer,1979). We must also remember that, "Food policies, therefore, must be concerned with balancing the interests of different groups in society so that food prices are consistent with a stabilized economy while also providing returns to farmers that will ensure a steady expansion of their output"(Chou & Harmon, 1979). We should therefore not be attacking only the visible areas that need attention, i.e., the high risk people for CHD or hypertensia patients, but the nation as a whole and as the nation's health is governed by the groups above, shouldn't they be concerned about the nation's health. "Given that western diseases are diet-related, that is to say caused in large part by food. Responsibility for their prevention largely passes from the hands of the doctors to government, industry and those responsible for health education... national change requires action at a national level"(Cannon & Walker,1984).

The government does need to take action and it was thought that, "when the government announced its intention in 1986 to review food law it was hoped that the opportunity would be taken to increase single tier enforcement authorities to bring greater order and uniformity to food law administration" (Painter,1990).

Though there are many interests involved in the setting of food laws and one group will have more power than another, we seriously need to consider the individual and their health.

To see the way forward we can look at countries which have adopted healthier eating habits to enable their nation to have good health. "Increases in cardiovascular disease, largely responsible for a 25 percent increase in medical expenditures over a 10 year period, was one of the principal reasons why Sweden developed a national nutrition policy" (Chou & Harmon,1979). Norway have also implemented such a policy and "agricultural policies have been adjusted to achieve optimum nutritional standards.

The plan encompasses food pricing and production policies to encourage Norwegians to adopt healthier eating habits: A diet composed of more vegetables, cereals, fish and poultry, and less red meat, saturated fat and sugar... In the United States, cereal enrichment has been a major factor contributing to the virtual elimination of vitamin deficiency... it seems essential that cereals continue to be enriched with those nutrients formerly obtained through meat" (Chou & Harmon,1979).

We must remember, however, that it is not just the industrialised countries that can show us the way forward in nutrition as many developing countries survive on little meat, yet are healthy people. It has also been documented that "India has done more research than the United States on fortification of salt with iron and how nutrition affects resistance to diseases, so we may learn as much from developing countries as industrialized ones" (Chou & Harmon, 1979).

Authors' Note in 2009: As you can see, lots of food laws and policies have been in place since the late 1970's, though it has taken until the millennium for advertisers to project that "we are what we eat." Thankfully, people such as Jamie Oliver were born during this period. He appears to be making his life's ambition as a chef, to produce healthy food for all, especially for children who will one day become the next adults.

Ainsley Harriott is another role model.

There have, however, been many food activists whom are lesser known, myself being one of them. As a former classroom assistant, actions of agitation could be clearly seen in certain sugar/additive driven children.

Since 2006 to date, I sit on two NHS health boards, whose mission is to improve the nations' health and offer people options on health alternatives in the health arena. The 2nd board looks at awareness in the field of Sickle Cell Anaemia.

I hope in the years to come, healthy lifestyles will become an everyday way of life for all.

Bibliography

Chou & Harmon, Ed. Critical Food Issues of the Eighties. Pergammon Press Ltd, England. 1979. Pgs 104,116.

Femten, Ed. Good Health - Is There a Choice? The Macmillan Press Ltd. 1981. London. pg5.

Fox & Cameron. Food Science, Nutrition and Health. Fifth Edition. Hodder & Stoughton. London 1989. pg2

Mayer & Dwyer, Ed. Food and Nutrition Policy in a Changing World. Oxford University Press. New York. 1979. Pg7.

Mills. The Politics of Dietary Change, Dartford Publishing Company Ltd. 1992. England. Pgs 97,101,135.

Painter. A. A. Ed. A Guide to the Food Safety Act 1990. Butterworths Law of Food and Drugs. Butterworths. 1990. London. pg17.

The Times 9th February 1991. Author ?

Walker & Cannon. The Food Scandal. Century Publishing, 1984. London. Pgs 1,2,5,6,156,159.

Whitehead Margaret Ed. The Health Divide, pgs 251, 332, 333,341, New Ed. Revised and Updated, Inequalities in Health, Penguin Books Ltd. London 1992

Mark awarded 68%

Preamble to Essay 7: According to official statistics women are over-represented in patient Mental Health Care and are twice as likely in comparison with men to be admitted for Neurosis. Outline possible reasons for this.

Mental health and well being is a subject area close to my heart. Upon completing my B.A, I furthered my learning by pursuing an M.A in Psychoanalytic Theory.

Essays such as the one that follows, fed my appetite to wish to know more in these fields, and also my desire to investigate why certain groups within society appear more likely to become labelled than others.

Statistics on Ethnicity and Race within mental health have been thought and debate provoking, as, according to recent figures 70% of Black and ethnic peoples will have some sort of mental health 'interaction' within their lifetime. Considering such people comprise only 6% of the population in Britain, this is highly worrying,

Will the passing of time bring change?

Hopefully such change will be for the betterment of all involved.

More information on this subject can be found within my first book, "Nubian Minds.". Stocked in most good book stores and online via www.tamarehouse.com/nubianminds

You will find, in what follows, my ideas and thoughts on why more women than men are admitted with the diagnosis of a Neurosis. You will see that many experiments in this field are on the basis of trial and error. Not great news if you are on the receiving end.

Women and their bodies have and still are the greatest "thing" to be investigated within the medical model. Creatures of curiosity and many moods, what makes women different from men is and has been a controversial discussion for many.

In the field of Psychiatry and mental health, the differences are not as clearly established as they might be. Men have initially been in positions of power and leadership within medical institutions long before women were considered viable students. With the advent of physiological and anatomical differentiation of women, some male physicians were so amazed at the fact that women had so many different parts to her that might affect her that many an experiment was performed just on a exploratory basis to test the circulating theories.

Electronic devices used to administer electric shocks were said to clear the mind and hysterectomies performed to heal the thought processes of women. The origin of the term Hysterectomy means, "removing the hysteria from woman."

It is only through thorough investigation and insight that the essay question can be fully responded to.

I hope the following insights into statistical knowledge and understanding of the terminology will help you expand your ideas of the issues that this essay addresses.

Essay 7:

According to official statistics women are over-represented in patient Mental Health Care and are twice as likely in comparison with men to be admitted for Neurosis. Outline possible reasons for this.

In order to answer the question being asked we first of all need to define its meaning. How are official statistics made up and what uses do they provide?
Reasons for women's overrepresentation in mental health care also need to be addressed.

"Official statistics are produced primarily to provide the information required by administrators, 'mandarins' (the very highest civil servants) and ministers in government departments. A secondary function of increasing importance is the provision of an information service to industry and commerce" (Hammersley, 1993:146).

So statistical data is something which is very much controlled by the state and is used in a variety of ways i.e., to see if homelessness is rising, whether ill health is on the increase in specific areas and what resources (financial) can be placed in which department.

"The methods and concepts developed and used for official statistics are shaped by the sorts of policies powerful people in the state wish to consider and by the concerns which preoccupy them. "These concerns, determine, at least partly, which phenomena are to be investigated as 'social problems' and which are neglected" (Hammersley, 1993:153). Therefore, if a minister or someone with such influence, has an interest in a certain field, investigation is more likely to be followed up, and as many ministers are male maybe this has something to do with the lack of government interest in this (mental health) largely female dominated field.

Hospital statistics are made up of counting the numbers of beds used in hospitals. Gender, age and marital status are often asked for on admission into the hospital. Government officials can then obtain this data and process it to see how one district compares to another district. Births, deaths and admittances into hospital are all calculated in the same way and areas of poor health etc. can be targeted more effectively by health officials. If this is true, what is happening in the mental health sector where the increase in women while mental disorders are not decreasing.

> *"In Britain, as in several other countries, women are very considerably overrepresented among mental hospital patients... the increased attention paid recently to sexual inequality in society has led to a refocusing of attention to this issue"* (Cochrane, 1983:40).

Could there be societal causes making this phenomena of increasingly sick women happen, i.e., low paid jobs? Holland (1989) says, "the explanation for sexual division in the labour market is that women have lower educational attainment and less training (particularly on the job) than men and so are only suitable for work in the secondary rather than in the primary sector" (Holland 1989). Women, therefore need to work almost twice as hard and still be responsible for the majority of the housework in order to have a better lifestyle.

The ideal picture of a woman, as advertised on television or in magazines, shows her doing the housework and maybe raising children yet she always has a smile on her face and everyone is shown in excessively clean clothes. In real life however this can be exhausting work, mentally as well as physically, for any person. Delphy and Leonard calculate approximately how much harder:

"The working week of a full-time housewife with children is still 60-80 hours in both rural and urban areas (although the working week for full-time male workers in industry has declined by about 10 hours, to 40 hours plus overtime)" (Delphy & Leonard, 1992).

Being looked upon by advertisements and daily life stereotypically as a "woman" or the 'second sex' as Simone de Beauvoir spoke of in 1952 and therefore always having to live in the shadow of man and not his equal. Feminists, suffragettes and others alike have been battling for years for women to be equal with men at home and in the workplace, yet historical factors about women still emerge today.

Showalter (1985) says that T.S Clouston, a Doctor in the 1870's believed that: "woman was constituted to be the helpmate and companion of man; her innate qualities of mind were formed to make her man's complement rather than his equal" (Showalter:123). Even if this view of woman was over a century ago, it still appears to be the case in today's society, as this next writer displays when describing womanhood.

> *"A woman's primary role is that of motherhood and most women have some or other of the attributes which fit them for this role.*

Consequently, the pursuit of a career for the mother of a young family is an arduous and conflict-ridden undertaking" (Hutt 1972:136). Woman's dependency on Man for financial and childrearing support subjects her to a more restrictive life which centres mainly on the home. In conjunction with what has been said, married women are more likely to be diagnosed with a mental illness than a man of the same status yet statistics (see appendix 1) show single men and divorced more prone to be inpatients for mental illness. Cochrane writes,

"it is only in the married category which accounts for the majority of the population, that women have higher rates of mental hospital admission" Cochrane 1983:45).Reasons for this will be discussed later after describing neurosis and how it is diagnosed.

Before the description, I would like to point out that males do have higher admission rates as in-patients between the ages of 0-14 (see Appendix 2), one reason could be that fixed gender patterns are established between these ages, according to psychologist Piaget and much confusion could arise if manly pursuits do not feel attractive to some boys. Even though this essay is about women being compared to men this point will not be discussed further due to space.

Oppression springs to mind when societies ideal of a person is to take second place and be happy with it. An unhappy woman may find an outlet in neurosis and hospital admission. In hospital everything is regulated i.e., mealtimes, the taking of medication and a woman could be said to find more time for herself.

This idea links in with a study done by Laing in the 1950's, which will be commented on later. If we now see what neurosis is, this will help build a picture of its easy connection to woman.

Neurosis is described in Drevers' Dictionary of Psychology as: "a functional disorder, psychogenic in origin, of the nervous system, the same as psychoneurosis; by psychoanalysts regarded as a conflict phenomenon, involving the thwarting of some fundamental instinctive urge." (Drever, 1952:185). Hence people labelled with this disorder are seen as unbalanced in the way in which they portray themselves.

Neurotic character described in Drever's dictionary leads you on to look at Adler's (a psychologist in the earlier part of this century) Masculine protest which is, "A term used by Adler as an equivalent for desire of superiority, or completeness, arising out of a felt inferiority, or incompleteness, femininity being regarded as incomplete and inferior" (Drever:164).

Women and her feminine ways are visibly discriminated against as man is seen as more complete in himself than woman.

Biological disposition is another area that needs to be questioned i.e., the idea that bodily malfunction cause women to be more susceptible than men.

Currently there are twice as many women with mental illness as compared to men, so a woman's biological workings, may be connected to her susceptibility to neurosis (which is diagnosed as a mental illness). This idea has been around throughout history. Hysteria was viewed by the Greeks as: "A functional disturbance of the nervous system - and attended with emotional disturbances or perversions of the moral and intellectual faculties.

"Women, being more liable than men to this disorder, it was originally thought to be due to a disturbance of the uterus" (Oakley 1985:76).

Menstruation, pre-menstrual tension, postnatal depression and the change of life are all biologically connected to woman and changes in her mood and behaviour have been documented by many leaflets readily available in clinics. A woman's uncertain ways is a topic well discussed in everyday life, yet she is penalised by being more easily categorised as neurotic, Allen writes that, "with stereotypical views about women in general - as unstable, irrational and changeable - statistical confirmation evokes little surprise" (Allen 1986:86).

However, if mental illness is biologically linked how is it that all women do not suffer from mental illness? A good percentage of men also suffer from mental illnesses too. According to Comer (1995), many people at some time in their lifetime suffer from what is commonly known as depression which can lead to neurosis. "It is estimated that as many as 17 percent of all adults in the world experience an episode of severe unipolar depression at some point in their lives" (Comer 1995:270).

This observation shows that biology is not connected, so sex is indiscriminate yet, woman's biological workings have for many centuries been connected with their behaviour. The history of women's illness is documented in much literature over the years, such as English and Ehnrereich's (1979) For Her Own Good, Showalter's (1987) The Female Malady, Women and Mental Illness by Miles (1989), to only name a few. Such books show how a woman's womb, menstruation or sometimes excessive emotional state is down to her biology.

A definition of neurosis has already been made so we shall look and see how Doctors define this disorder as compared to other disorders. This may throw light on why twice as many women than men are placed into this category, hence boosting female figures.

Depression which can lead to neurosis comes in various forms and postnatal/partum depression is exclusively attached to women, namely new mothers. An interview by

Dalton (1996) shows the distress some women feel at this point in their lives.

A woman wrote:

"I break down into floods of tears in the street, shops and other inconvenient places'" (Dalton et. al:57). Personal experience has shown that in-patient care for new mothers is usually given by prolonging the mothers stay or releasing her and readmitting her shortly afterwards.

Women often talk to friends, social workers or GPs if they do not feel 'right' within themselves. a study by Gurin et al. assessing general adjustment, indicated that 'women expressed more worrying, more often felt they had experienced a nervous breakdown, and more often felt they had a personal problem that could have benefited from professional help' (Gurin et al. 1960:41; Evans et al. 1983:115).

So far we have seen that women appear more emotional than men and speak up about it, and that they are labelled by most of society as carers within society more than man's equal partner. People usually portray their gendered behaviour patterns according to what sex they are, and "normal healthy behaviour differs for men and women" (Evans et al.1983:121).

Oakley writes on a study done in 1978 by Barrett & Roberts, they studied consulting patterns of GPs and found that a women's anxiety and 'depression' was caused mainly by their inadequate adjustment to domesticity, and that 'readjustment' to domesticity was the treatment (Oakley,1981:79). Psychotropic drugs such as valium are then dispensed "for, if medical treatment does not cure... it is a way of exercising control over the social functions of women... ensuring that women conform in practice to the image of femininity that is the stereotyped ideal" (Oakley:79). It appears that if women are not oppressed by the patriarchal system then the drugs will get them to perform correctly. Reasons for why women have higher rates in one area and men in another can be seen below.

> *"Women tend to have higher rates, both for in-patient and general practitioner contact, for neurosis, and affective disorders... Psychopathy, drug abuse, alcoholism, sexual deviation, drug- and alcohol-induced psychoses... are all more common among male patients." Women predominate in the psychiatric disorders related to emotion and men towards behaviour related disorders (Evans et. al., 1983:118).*

Men therefore are less likely to be placed in the emotional statistics for neurosis. Boverman et.al (1970) studied how clinicians diagnosed patients using stereotypical views as foundations "this study showed that clinicians' stereotypes of a mentally healthy women differed from their stereotype of a mentally healthy man - the latter was closer to that for the overall ideal of adult mental health" (Evans et al:121), even in the diagnostic category women are already viewed as a lesser stereotypical adult. Men however, are socialised differently from women and are trained if not at home then by the system i.e., choosing male subjects at school, attending football/rugby matches, pub crawling etc. or doing other manly pursuits. Name calling such as sissy and poof can be heard in most playgrounds and serve (maybe unknowingly to the child) as reinforces that divide the two sexes. Sociologists and psychologists are constantly trying to unravel why people do what they do and a person's socialisation usually comes into the investigation somewhere along the line.

One sociologist of the 1950's Talcott Parsons, views the family from a nuclear perspective and sees the fathers' role within this model as a breadwinner and disciplinarian, with the mothers role being dependent on her spouse, the caregiver for him and the children hence a balance in life is supposedly created for all.

Parsons says "the modern family deals with the socialization of children and gives stability to adult personalities" (Abercrombie & Warde 1994:271), modern statistics prove this latter part incorrect as previously shown more married women than men become unstable during marriage and having children. We must remember that more single parent families are in today's society unlike in Parsons era and women have needed to learn how to bring a child/ren up on their own hence more pressure of daily life is placed upon them. Stress and anxiety are seen as connecting factors towards mental illness.

The diagnosis of neurosis shows us that emotional labels are mainly used and as women demonstrate more of these labels in everyday life than men, higher numbers of being treated and needed to be looked after as hospital in-patients will emerge in statistical figures.

Allen (1986) says "this relative excess of women occurs across almost all the diagnostic categories of psychiatry, with the exception of alcoholism and personality disorder, but is most marked in relation to depression and psycho neuroses" (1986:85).

A new mother talked to Dalton and said she had loss of emotional control and unable to stop certain behaviour patterns, these patterns are viewed by doctors and others, yet some women do not know why they reacted so strangely in situations they would not normally have done so, as a mother myself feeling anxious about your new child's welfare is something all concerned parents feel.

Everyday sayings such as "just like a woman, always changing her mind", reinforce stereotypical views.

Psychiatrists also need to form a view, feminist writers such as Allen say that "The scales are already unbalanced at the moment of expectation; psychiatrists approach women with assumptions about female mentality that may condition what they 'see' and influence how they respond" (Allen 1986:96), and as the psychiatric field is dominated by men, how many unfair judgements are made?

The famous R.D Laing study done between 1951-56 at a hospital in Glasgow, shows how a woman's surroundings i.e., family, social situation can all place stress and cause illness within the person.

Laing segregated a number of women who had been diagnosed as schizophrenic and gave them a comfortable living space, he found after a while that these women improved greatly and therefore sent them home, within a period of months all the women had been readmitted either by themselves or their families. It appears from this story that independence from family ties, housework etc. gave the women hope and they could organise themselves better as in-patients. This may be another factor for high in-patient statistics.(Bush, 1994, Lecture notes).

If we now conclude on what has been written, we can see that statistics are monitored by and for a mainly male government, whose first interest of help may not be directed towards a mainly dominated female area. Also physicians, psychiatrists, GPs etc. all have preconceived views on how it is to be a woman and stereotypical literature/media does not give woman her due as much more positive roles could be portrayed through the advertisers, media and television.

Woman's' dependence on man as the sole family breadwinner is slowly evolving as more women work now than ever before, hence independence amongst more successful women may show in the future.

Another question that also needs to be considered is, if men were as oppressed as women in any given society, would high numbers of neurotic or mentally ill men overtake women?, Cochrane writes

> *"equally there are societies, and indeed ethnic groups within our society, where the pattern is reversed... This is true in the Republic of Ireland and in Scotland" (1983:45).*

War and bombings have been rife for many years in parts of Ireland, and maybe men feel oppressed and obliged by the government and society to fight for their country.

Scotland according to hearsay has a high rate of drug users and poverty, so "Although there are very affluent areas in Scotland and the North, there is also the greatest concentration of material deprivation" (Whitehead 1992 pg251). Such reasons could become valid observations for resetting the standard of mental health labels.

A way forward for the future is given by Allen, she believes that a feminist politics should be adapted and quotes that, these politics according to Eichenbaum & Orbach say "we suggest that therapists ask themselves... How do they understand the woman's distress, what does this distress have to do with the experience of being a woman?, How is her gender central to what she is experiencing" (Allen:104). Maybe then, more understanding can be made of high in patient statistics, and even in this male dominated sphere of psychiatry "a feminine politics is not necessarily bound to fail: there may be real and achievable gains through seeking to raise the consciousness of the mental health professionals; seeking to develop and propagate methods of treatment that counteract rather than compound the disadvantages of women patients" (Allen:111)

Pass Mark 72%

Authors Note 2009

Can you imagine the many women whose lives have been intruded upon and backed by law?

A most horrifying and frustrating thought indeed.

In today's world, Women are still being admitted to mental health hospitals in great numbers along with Black people. If we are portraying care for all citizens then we need to find a more inclusive/interactive ways to change our minds from illness to wellness.

Bibliography

Abercrombie N & Warde A (1994) Contemporary British Society 2nd Ed. Polity Press:271.

Allen H (1986) The Power of Psychiatry; Psychiatry and the Construction of the Feminine, Polity, London.85-111.

Barrett M & Roberts H (1978) Doctors and their patients: the social control of women in general practice in Smart and Smart (eds.) (1978) Women, Sexuality and Social Control, Routledge and Kegan Paul, London.

Boverman et.al. (1970) Sex-role stereotypes and Clinical Judgements of Mental Health. Journal of Consulting and Clinical Psychology. 34:1-7.

Cochrane R, (1983) The Social Creation of Mental Illness, Longman, London.:40,45.

Comer, R.J (1995) Abnormal Psychology 2nd Edition. W.H Freeman & Co. London. 269-309.

Dalton, K & Holton, W. Depression after Childbirth: How to recognize treat, and prevent postnatal depression. Third Edition. Oxford University Press. Oxford. 13, 57

De Beauvoir S (1952), The Second Sex, Penguin Books. Lomdon.

Delphy C & Leonard D, (1992) Familiar Exploitation: an analysis of marriage in contemporary western societies Blackwell Publishers. London.

Drever J. (1952). A Dictionary of Psychology, Penguin Books, United Kingdom: 126,230.

Evans & Ungerson (1983) (eds.) Sexual Divisions: Patterns and Processes, Tavistock Publications, London.

Ehrenreich & English (1979) For Her Own Good: 150 years of the experts advice to women, Pluto Press Ltd. London.

Holland J, (1989) The social contexts of schooling, what is Gender?: Gender in Britain Today, Leves Falmer.

Hutt C (1972) Males & Females, Penguin Books, London.

Miles A (1989) Women & Mental Illness, Wheatsheaf, Brighton

Oakley A. (1982), Subject Women, Fontana Press, Great Britain, 76

Showalter E. The Female Malady, Woman, Madness and English Culture 1830-1980 (1985) Virago Press Ltd. London

Whitehead Margaret Ed. (1992), The Health Divide, in Inequalities in Health, Revised and Updated, New Ed, Penguin Books Ltd. London: 251,

References

Laing R.D quoted by Bush Tracy, (1994) Lecturer on Access Course.

Piaget (1971) quoted from Kurt Danzigers Socialization. Penguin Books Ltd. London

1Even though women have had to cope with bringing up children single-handedly during other periods of history i.e., during and after wars, kin relations appeared to be closer so more help was at hand.

Preamble to Essay 8: Discuss S. de Beauvoir's argument on the relationship between 'the woman' and 'otherness'

I clearly remember writing this essay and was pleased with the pass mark. Coming across such writers as Simone de' Beauvoir opened a whole new world to me and many others of my 1960s generation.

Looking back and re reading my work brings back the joy of discovering, as a young woman, that my own life contained choices. It really was exciting to learn that what I had considered ordinary free will had actually been fought long and hard for by women of many generations past.

Reading her work "The Second Sex" was liberation, expressed in words.

Simone lived with her man, unmarried, in a time when such women were not regarded as the greatest of role models. In fact, parents in the 1960/70s may probably have done their best to keep their daughters/sons away from writings and ideas such as this. Her lifestyle was certainly not the status quo at the time.

Now, in a completely different century, certain rules and regulations no longer apply, women can do practically anything they like, much more than in the time period written about in this essay. See for yourself how and why times have had to change.

We give thanks. I am extremely grateful for the sacrifices of women such as these. It is they who have enabled works like mine to be produced. In order to be read by you.

Essay 8:
Discuss S. de Beauvior's argument on the relationship between 'the woman' and 'otherness'

Simone de Beauvior makes a connection with woman and otherness by expressing her thoughts from everyday events. She believes women should go out into the world and seek their destiny on their own if they choose to.

Simone's argument is that woman is represented in universally as the other instead of the one, Man is seen as the one and the woman as the other his carer or attendant to enable him to have the best possible life chances i.e., job wise, health wise etc. He is the main provider for his wife and children's future. Woman is therefore seen as the bystander of life, not born to seek her liberty which Simone suggests she should be doing. Woman is born just as man; she breathes the same air why should her position be of a lower status. Literature and the media expand on this thought by deeming everything male,

"Man represents both the positive and the neutral, as it is indicated by the common use of man to designate human beings in general" (de Beauvoir 1952).

Should woman be born only to serve and live a second-hand existence? We seem to have been pushed somehow into the background whilst man is in the forefront, how did this come about? Why are women only channelled to do certain jobs and not others? Even when women do get the same job as men that particular profession is somehow degraded and equal pay is unlikely, I shall be detailing these questions and also why there appears to be a connection with mental health illness and women, this seems to affect more married women with children than anyone else. With woman being biologically equipped to carry and bear children the tag carer is easily attached,

> *"childcare is seen as a natural extension and concomitant of childbearing"*(Holland 1989), *has man forgotten that we could not bear children without his sperm, effectively the child is made up of both parents sets of genes. Once the woman has a child rest is need after the birth and so staying at home until the child is old enough to be looked after,(usually by another woman) has been the solution. If a woman decides to go back to work her job which is probably one of lower pay,*

I say this because when Goldthorpe did his study of social mobility only men were used as not enough women could be found of the same status also many of them work part-time to fit in with family duties. The main areas of work for the majority of women are jobs such as clerical work, catering and any other low profile jobs an explanation given by human capitalists says "The explanation for sexual division in the labour market is that women have lower educational attainment and less training (particularly on the job) than men and so are only suitable for work in the secondary rather than in the primary sector" (Holland 1989)

This statement clearly shows how woman is thought of as secondary, if the job is secondary there is no doubt the wages will be so also, (light can be seen at the end of the dark tunnel as more girls than boys received higher A level grades according to News at Ten last year). As child care has become extremely expensive especially if more than one child is concerned and the fact that nursery or childminding facilities are not heavily supported by the state even though a new law was introduced last year to give financial help enabling women's return ability to her job there is usually no other option except that the woman should stay at home and become a housewife and give full attention to her family. Morals and laws dictated through religion, the law and the state are also something which keeps the sexes unbalanced.

"Both the state and the legal system tend to support the sexual division of labour and the basic patriarchal paradigm of the dependant women and the breadwinner man." (Holland 1989)

Women are capable of doing "men's work" and have been called out to do this in times of national crisis such as in the war periods, they were used in factories to manufacture ammunition, trained as lorry drivers so deliveries could be sent out to necessary areas. Women also worked in aircraft engineering and became very skilled in many areas, however as soon as the war was over and men returned home from the trenches women were once again put back in their place, the home.

Being a housewife consists of economically non productive but necessary work such as washing, cleaning, cooking etc. All these tasks take up time and effort in fact women in most cases work longer hours than men.

> " The working week of a full-time housewife with children is still 60-80 hours in both rural and urban area's (although the working week for full-time male workers in industry has declined by about 10 hours, to 40 hours plus overtime)" (Delphy and Leonard 1992)

With woman being so occupied with so many demands, when does she find time to be or find herself? How did women gain this position? One of the lecturers at the university gives an example of why men became the head of household and not woman. Engles traced it back to hunting and gathering societies in which gender divisions appear not to exist, though men gather as do the women it is only men who are allowed to hunt, this rule is used for safety's sake. As men started to herd large amounts of cattle or surplus meat supply, the surplus was then used to trade for goods and later on property could be gained. This wave of progression in turn lead to more properties and factories being built consequently change brought along with it male bosses and women were dispensed with into the home. This theory demonstrates flaws however, firstly it assumes that woman will politely go into a home without talking to her husband about being involved in the business side of things, after all she must have noticed a change in her lifestyle and surroundings. Secondly around 1830 which was not so long after the enlightenment the women's suffragette movement started to campaign for legal rights for women, and thirdly

"The nature of early society can never be constructed with complete confidence; nevertheless, the hunter-gatherer data should make us view with suspicion any theory that seeks to prove that the male dominance in our present social order is a part of an evolutionary heritage" (Meggary 1995).
If a woman remains within the confines of the home day after day frustration and boredom will inevitably set in, she has not only lost her financial independence by not working but friendships that were formed within the working environment, maybe she will try to make friends with a neighbour, or the close friends you do have go to work, but how much can you trust a new person? Especially if I don't want the entire neighbourhood knowing my business, thoughts such as these can enter your head, Laurie says on this subject

> *"Most mothers of small children live on new estates where people do not know each other. Locked in their brick boxes, the women distrust each other, and become friendless, exhausted, dispirited"* (Laurie 1974) *isolation and fear of not being good for much other than housework is enough to lower anyone's self-esteem.*

"Part of the system's technique for keeping women apart is to set up extraordinary standards of cleanliness and hygiene by which they are judged" (Laurie 1974) many people and institutions such as the RSPCA think it is cruel to keep a dog locked up all day!!!.

Our socialisation method plays a big part of our adult life, even if as children we grew up knowing which gender role to take on because it has been defined by our sex. Certain colours are usually nominated to be either, male or female, masculine or feminine, bold stern blues and greys for boys and pale soft pinks and yellows for girls, times are however changing and unisex clothes and colours have been introduced onto the market for a number of years now. At some point in our lives we learn which characteristics are accepted and which are not, a boy playing with dolls and showing some sort of affection is seen as girlish behaviour and is sure to be ridiculed in the playground, whereas a girl wanting to play football or climb trees is seen as being tomboyish, however the girl is less likely to be less ridiculed in that situation as she is seen as wanting to be like a boy or the first sex.

"Boys are brought up to be aggressive, virile, to lay anything. Women are trained to be passive, to wait to be chosen, to make an effort to please in every situation" (Laurie 1974)

What if we don't want to be chosen or pleasing to men but follow our own intuitions, stereotypical labels such as frigid, weirdo or lesbian are readily attached, if a woman wanted to lay anything just as her counterparts seem to, slag, whore and any other derogatory names are fetched out of the man's conscious cupboard and used for mental ammunition. Men universally are conscious of the fact that they are (or have deemed themselves to be seen in such a way that this is reflected in everyday life) the first sex, this makes them the leaders and women the followers, the female creation would not be around if it was not for Adam.

Simone depicts in her writing by such levels of action in that man can do as he wishes but woman should do as she is told,

"Man can think of himself without woman. She cannot think of herself without man."

Woman does have a lot to contend with, knowing she is as competent as man though his physical strength does exceed our own. The feelings of being trapped in a situation you predicted to be wonderful i.e., marriage, but in reality was not so great could leave you feeling depressed and as Silverman states "There appear to be no exceptions to the generalization that depression is more common in women than in men, whether it is the feeling of depression, neurotic depression, or depressive psychosis" (Silverman 1968).

During socialisation as previously talked about, girls are treated differently than boys but they are still accepted as part of the family, who laugh, cry, catch measles etc., and feel loved and wanted. If you then grow up and enter into marriage or co-habitation were everything is wonderful in the beginning until boredom and routine set in, finding yourself rocking a distressed baby and trying to entertain a demanding toddler is hard work especially if it seems you never get a break from it. Whitehead calls this the 'ideology of maternal altruism' that "leads a woman to put the family or children first. Showalter also expresses this when she says "Woman of all social classes complained more of stress and unhappiness in marriage than their male peers" (Showalter 1985).

As Holland says when the woman does go and seek advice from someone she feels is qualified to help, she pays the GP a visit and is usually given anti-depressants and or psychotic drugs which supposedly block out the stress factor, women users I have talked to say it makes them feel spaced out and nervous about not being in control. If a woman goes back to her GP because she doesn't feel the tablets are helping her situation, some women are prescribed Electroconvulsive therapy (ECT) which is a series of electric shocks to the brain. An American Dr called Peter Breggin says on this subject

"ECT, he maintains is recommended for the less skilled persons whose livelihoods are not dependant on the use of memory and intellect: housewives can be seen as excellent candidates on these terms" (Showalter 1985).

To summarise on the information gathered, I do not believe woman has lost her way but followed misleading male signs like waiting for Mr Right etc. A woman's (or females) life should not be predetermined with the view that she will marry (though not necessarily the case nowadays), bear children and look after her husband and family. There are other things in life that she is or could be capable of, if male boundary lines which have been formed by a patriarchal system were removed or adjusted to make it universally a lot fairer for both sexes to enjoy their lives.

With the disappearance of many manual jobs that supported the state or country in a big financial or beneficial way for many decades ,and had a high ratio of male employers such as the coal miners, steelworkers, the railway industry etc. A wider opening into the job market for women is through development in technology. Technological advancement gives way to the physical strength aspect and so one area of discrimination will be eliminated. Also now more women are returning to higher education and as Ann Oakley phrases it "Education was the golden door, the automatic escape from second-class citizenship. Twentieth-century feminists cherish a similar vision, and have attached a similar importance to the right of equal education as the necessary strategy for freeing women from the 'ideological prison' of femininity" (Oakley 1981)

68% pass mark

Bibliography

Simone de Beauvoir, The second sex (1952) Penguin

Christine Delphy and Diana Leonard, Familiar Exploitation, an analysis of marriage in contemporary western societies(1992) Blackwell Publishers. London.

Janet Holland, The social contexts of schooling, what is Gender: Gender in Britain Today, (1989) Leves:Falmer

Peter Laurie, Meet your friendly social system (1974)

Diana Leonard and John Hood-William's, Families, issues in sociology, (1988) Macmillan Education Ltd. London

Elaine Showalter, The Female Malady, Woman, Madness and English Culture 1830-1980 (1985) Virago Press Ltd

References

News at Ten

Lecturer Floya Athinas

103

<u>Footnotes</u>

As the majority of countries world-wide have patriarchal systems the term universal will be used to represent the majority.
"Certain universal functions define the institution, the functions are universal,
Therefore, the institution is universal. If too wide a definition is accepted, the whole debate is pointless." (Is the family universal)
A housewives work is not seen as a job in the eyes of the state but more of a choice "she can work if she really wants or needs to." A single woman would find it difficult to own or buy her own property as her wages are found to be lower than that of a mans, if women were paid wages for doing 90% of the household chores it would cost the country billions of pounds a year, this blatant action by the system means
"the inability of single women to get mortgages, and of women in general to follow careers as fully as men" Laurie then goes on to say
"Altering the cohabitation rule would free women at a stroke from dependence on men, would free men from subjection to women and would lose the system its most diligent enforcer: the housewife" Laurie, Woman, Sex and pain.

<u>Authors note 2009</u>

I clearly remember writing this essay and was pleased with the pass mark. Looking back and re reading my work brings back the joy of discovering as a young woman that my life contained choices. It really was exciting to learn that what I had considered ordinary free will had actually been fought long and hard for by women of many generations past.

We give thanks and I am extremely grateful for their sacrifices in order for works like mine to be produced.

Preamble to Essay 9: Final Year Dissertation 1996-97. The View of Autonomy as Spoken by Wheelchair Users in 1997 Historical Theoretical Perspectives

This is my Dissertation for my B.A in Sociology and Psychology. It felt great to be finally nearing the end of my 3 year degree journey.

Reviewing this work takes me back to when I was raising 4 small children (who were all under 10) one of which being severely disabled, a quadriplegic. Most days I felt like I had done a day's work before going into University lectures! Yet I knew then, as now, that you can achieve anything you put your mind and body to.

I was also motivated to attend each day by knowing I would, at the end gain letters after my name and wear the mortar with gown once I had graduated.

It was the need to explore how life might become for my disabled son, Benjamin who inspired me to write and investigate the area of wheelchair users. I remember a time in my life when I pushed a twin buggy and a wheelchair, though how I achieved this at the time has since intrigued me.

In this dissertation, I interviewed 3 wheelchair users who allowed me to take a look into their personal lives and then go on to produce this piece of work. I thank them for this and often wonder how they are doing now 12 years later. Hopefully they are enjoying the many new wheelchair access places and opportunities this may have opened for them. I thank them for their time and energy and willingness to share and shed light on a much deserved issue.

The main theorists views used in this research are found in Len Doyal and Ian Goughs' book: A Theory of Human Need (1991). My research tools are a questionnaire and life histories taken from the above book plus many other books and theories as well as the aforementioned interviewees, who showed me what it was to experience and observe such theories in action.

Exploring how or if theoretical knowledge can become a real life phenomenon intrigued me to the point of wanting to gain further knowledge in this area and use it in my own life at an advantage.

The book, 'A Theory of Human Need' gave me insights into the needs of all human beings and their rights to be considered normal. This statement goes against how we lived in 1997.

What I mean by this is that it was impossible to push a wheelchair or buggy onto a London bus or Tube at that time. Now in 2009 we have seen a new era emerge as able and disabled bodies can take themselves to their destinations with more ease than before, though challenges still exist, therefore enhancing the lives of many wheelchair users.

This dissertation can be seen as being ahead of its time, as suggestions to overhaul or make good trains and buses for wheelchair users have since been introduced.

Hopefully as a society, we will grow to love and help all people, whatever our abilities, expanding our thoughts and actions as we go along. An old saying goes, "each one, teach one" these are true words indeed.

Essay 9:
Final Year Dissertation 1996-97. The View of Autonomy as Spoken by Wheelchair Users in 1997. Historical Theoretical Perspectives

A persons' autonomy or self governing of their own lives has been viewed by many sociologists and sometimes psychologists as a very important feature for the development of human existence universally.

How do we perceive what we see, hear or feel and why do we do this?, theorists such as Hamilton 1993, Piaget and Giddens etc. all give answers to such questions.

Since individuals are a part of a society or group interacting with others, the structure of that society has to be recognised in order to get a clearer picture of how the individual sees themselves and the restrictions or limits placed on them from the outside world.

This essay will be mainly concerned about western views on the structured society. My theoretical perspective will be based on writers such as Durkheim, Marx and Weber all written on the subject of human enclosure groups and the mechanisms of society.

The main theorists views used in this research are found in Len Doyal and Ian Goughs' book A Theory of Human Need (1991). It has given me an insight into the needs of all human beings. However trying to assess needs and wants can be difficult and they say, "Theory and practice which are critical of the political and moral status quo could equally well start with the more positive image of fundamental human 'flourishing' and refer to the different sorts of social environments which encourage and sustain this process" (Doyal and Gough, 1991:2).

I am interested in finding out if peoples' surroundings (i.e., lifestyle, relationships) make a difference to how they perceive themselves in ways of positiveness etc. in how they live their lives and also how much and if a wheelchair (WC) stops them from having a life they would like.

So if we look for differences in wheelchair users being positive within their lives (i.e., whether they work or would like to? are they in a relationship with a partner, and autonomy of self (i.e., how included they feel in societies structure), we can help merge a better way forward for integration as the disabled are also people of the future. Disabled people have been viewed negatively in the past, such as "less than whole... a threat, objects of ridicule, pitiful or eternal children" (Barnes,1990:158). Different styles of living i.e., communicating with picture boards, through computers or other aids is not something done openly in mainstream schools or work institutions hence such restrictions on being visible may disallow them to live their own lives as they may wish.

What rights or say do many disabled people have in their style of life? What measures are being taken now politically and socially, and what plans are indicated for the future?

Is a positive picture beginning to emerge for the up and coming children labelled disabled or will they face the same negativeness of societies views as their previous counterparts.

As my main concern is putting across only wheelchair users (WU) views, I cannot go into detail about all disabilities.

Historical sociological perspectives are important when looking at the future, as inequalities of some kind amongst human beings have always existed.

Durkhiem has written about what he calls moral regulations, these are social regulators such as the legal system, education system, etc., and says they are all needed to keep man happy, regulated and give him a form of direction in his life. Without regulation Durkheims says man will be lost and qualities such as greediness, no morals, selfishness and total self interest will be mans main objective instead of learning to think about others and their needs

"Thus, the more one has, the more one wants, since satisfactions received only stimulate instead of filling needs... But since the individual has no way of limiting them, this must be done by some force exterior to him" (Durkheim, Ed. Thompson & Tunstall:111.

However as people cannot be physically forced to think in a manner which benefits all, Durkheim says "A regulative force must play the same role for moral needs which the organism plays for physical needs. This means that the force can only be moral" (:111). An equilibrium between some men having all and others nothing needs to be constructed within society for everyone to benefit "it is not enough for the average level of needs for each social condition to be regulated by public opinion, but another, more precise rule must fix the way in which these conditions are open to individuals with unfair and unseen restrictions.

If we look at Marx's views on livelihoods we can see that public opinion matters immensely for people's well-being. Marx argued that a persons' position in society mattered, as some people have more personal benefits than others. Marx was in favour of equality for all, equal pay, equal rights whereby all people can choose how they live and not be restricted by where they stood on the mode of production line. Disabled people can be said to have a similar unequal position in society as discrimination in the workplace deems the disabled as unseen, unemployable beings.

Factory workers on a production line for instance, form relationships with each other in the workplace and this socialisation could develop into social friendships, Marx would call this situation "a class in itself" as they were all of a similar status job wise or from social interaction, "social circumstances in which the activity of individuals occurs condition their perception of the world in which they live"(Giddens 1971)

Certain peoples experiences and life chances to become "free" are limited when shackled with unnecessary bias.

Introduction

The original title of this paper was, The Autonomous Self as Viewed by the Wheelchair Bound in the London Borough of Greenwich. My first step was to place advertisements for interviewees in a newsletter which is run by the women's' centre at Hare Street, Woolwich, I was stopped in my tracks by the woman (Louisa Golding) on the other end of the telephone as I informed her of my plight.

After explaining what I was looking for she replied "We can't place wheelchair-bound in the advertisement... as the terminology is incorrect and offensive, due to the fact, that a person's facilitator i.e., wheelchair is just a prop that is needed to enable an individual to become mobile and should not be seen as a prohibitor" (Oliver Oct 96)

I replied that "I did not mean to be offensive by using everyday terminology and was sorry."

At that point the conversation went on and Louisa and I placed the ad ready for the Nov\Dec issue of Women in Greenwich Newsletter. Politically Correct (PC) language sprung to mind, this is something I had touched on in certain courses previously and will be included within this essay.

The Greenwich carers centre also placed an ad for me, but terminology was not a problem with them and it was placed its original form. Language is an important part of our everyday life, and the meanings which become attached to a particular form of language. Hugman (1991) says that

"Language is a central aspect of discourse through which power is reproduced and communicated" (Hugman:37), PC has been introduced into the language sphere and how to express words in a (PC) way is on the increase, as indicated by my telephone conversation.

The term wheelchair-bound suggests that the individual is tied to the chair and is therefore not seen as an individual with other qualities.

An advertisement was also placed in a Unicef chemist opposite Greenwich Hospital and at the Greenwich Advice for the Disabled, otherwise known as the GAD office. As I did not receive a great response from Greenwich wheelchair residents, a decision was made to expand this opportunity to all wheelchair users responding.

The last date to apply for interviews was set at 10th Dec 1996, however my son was admitted to hospital for a planned operation on 4th Nov. and two weeks was the recovery time which had been discussed with Ben's Drs.

Unplanned complications emerged and a second operation needed to be performed, as my son is not physically strong, recovery took over a month, hence all interviewees ringing did not make contact with me and all my work connected with this dissertation needs to be rescheduled.

There was however light at the end of the tunnel as my son recovered and a man named Geoff Carlton rang me up in early January, and told me he knows the date for application is past but could he help me out in any way.

He told me that he was not a wheelchair user but worked with wheelchair users in the sports field. Mr Carlton has offered me a trip to Lympe Farm, which is used for respite care and creative activities for wheelchair users and the disabled.

I took Mr Carltons offer and the date of the male interviews discussed in this paper was 22nd March 1997. Tracey Bishops interview was conducted on 20th April 1997. These life stories were gained using ethnographic research, and my appreciation is given to the interviewees for taking up this offer of an encounter with a stranger.

During this essay disability will be seen as that described by Prof. Mike Oliver in lectures 1996, "as a loss or limitation of opportunities to take part in the normal life of the community on an equal level with others due to physical and social barriers" (Oliver,1996)

A physical disability or a wheelchair is very symbolic in the way that it distracts or attracts people's attention, and Jenny Morris states how these personal symbols may be interpreted by others. "One of the biggest problems for disabled people is that all these undermining messages, which we receive every day of our lives from the non-disabled world which surrounds us, becomes part of our way of thinking about ourselves" (Morris 1996:75).

An interview done by Tom Shakespeare with a woman who was a wheelchair user, and sex was one of the topics that emerged, the woman told him that "A close friend assumed that, for me, sex was a thing of the past. I think this is a view shared by the majority. It may have little reality, but influences my self-image" Barton, 1996:193.

Images, stigmatisation's and stereotypes all play a part in society, certain groups of people can be stereotyped into something that is not true. If a person is visualised as someone to be pitied how do they find ways of being autonomous or self-governing.

Autonomous is described in the Little Oxford Dictionary 1986 as "self-governing" (1986:32), but self governing of which particular area in life is not stated.

Contemporary Theorists Doyal & Gough (1991), also have a description of autonomy and what they feel it consists of.

They have devised a theory which divides autonomy and physical health into one section for health and three main sections for autonomy with Restricted Participation being the main heading.

Figure 9.1 The relation between participation, health and autonomy

Restricted participation

Physical Disease	Mental Illness	Cognitive Deprivation	Restricted opportunities
	No Views		

These writers say that in order for an individual to reach goals they must be aware of the goals in the first place, and also of any 'serious harm' which is described as "significantly impaired pursuit of goals which are deemed of value by individuals. To be seriously harmed is thus to be fundamentally disabled in the pursuit of one's vision of the good" (:50)

Doyal & Gough therefore explain why this is part of their theory, and continue to say that "by our theory - the avoidance of serious harm regarded as the fundamental and sustained impairment of social participation - and the basic needs for physical health and autonomy. These needs were seen to be the universal conditions for achieving this goal (:171).

Disability as we described earlier can cause restricted participation within society, and as Oliver says physical and social barriers can be prohibitors.

If we firstly look at physical disease, which is under the health heading and then move onto the other sections, we can see how they affects a persons' autonomy.

When an individual is considered sick or in ill health, Drs and medical staff from all spheres i.e, GPs, analysts' psychiatrists etc. follow the medical model.

The medical model or individual as described by Oliver (1996), dictates that disabled people can be "put right" or made more normalised with the help of medical professionals. Medics try to change the person inwardly, i.e., by prescribing medicines or treatments that may help them. Doyal & Gough say "that approaches to theorising physical disease and illness can and do vary. Yet unless we are dealing with relatively minor diseases and illnesses where recovery is fairly certain... curative therapy has not proved especially effective, 'traditional' approaches find it hard to compete with medicine based on the biochemical model." (Doyal & Gough:175).

Oliver (1996) says that the medical approach indicates to society that the disabled person is the problem/burden, and that they need to be looked after by society in homes or institutions and hospitals instead of being integrated with the rest of society, their disability is seen as a personal tragedy, which they and their families must carry. Gillian Parker says "Sir Roy Griffiths Agenda for Action on community care stated that families, friends, neighbours and other local people would continue to be the primary means by which people are enabled to live normal lives in community settings" (Griffiths, 1988; Parker 1994:251), hence the disability is seen as the persons own fault and support from government bodies denied. Even if a person cannot take part physically, the mental satisfaction and stimulation they could gain may help give outlooks on life that they are denied when behind closed doors.

The Doyal & Gough theory being used to scale autonomy contains a section on mental illness; this section will not be used within these works as all three interviewees were competent. Cognitive depravation will therefore be the first element of this theory, and it could be said that if a person lacks communicative integration, events going on around them may become misunderstood by the individual whose cognition is blurred.

"Clearly the capacity for thinking about and doing new things must be contextualised in relation to the practical demands on [a] particular individual... To the degree, that an individual's patterns of learning, conform to such specific demands, his autonomy will be either helped or hindered" (182).

A person must understand what is happening around them and show enough enthusiasm to join in, but what of the severely disabled or others with communication difficulties. In this time close to the millennium, computer usage is rife and the Internet network is making it easier for computer users to access information from all over the world. There are many designs available and if the severely disabled could be taught from early on in their schooling days to use a button or switch to communicate and be seen by others as possible participators in life, their learning experiences would become greater and confidence could be built on. Welch says "Disabled people must be allowed and encouraged to exercise their skills and knowledge, not just in personal and domestic interactions but in as broad a context as possible. Experience is a learning process as well as a framework of reference and this enhances self-confidence and decision making" (Welch 1996:21).

Schooling and education are seen as an important part of becoming an adult as good education is vital nowadays to gain a well paid job.

Hales (1996) says "Disabled people were largely 'written off' and there were no expectations, or low expectations, of what disabled children and adults would achieve. It is only over the last 10 years or so that any real and meaningful attempts have been made to rescue disabled people from institutionalisation" (:6) hence integration is needed in schools and colleges and less barriers used restrict special needs pupils from the outside world.

The above statement ties in with Doyal and Gough's theory of restricted opportunity. How much opportunity was given for the disabled to integrate within society, when you do not have similar surroundings i.e., in institutions time is an element which everyone runs by. For example nurses care attendants etc. change shifts, meals are served at specified times along with medication, bedtime happens when lights go out irrespective to the degree of tiredness one might have.

A woman named Ruth Sienkiewicz - Mercer (1989) talks of her life in an institution, in her autobiography she talks of new attendants who were "lazy, disorganised, insensitive, impatient... they decided that it would be easier to feed me while I was lying flat on my back. This only made it harder for me to eat. It was also particularly boring to spend my whole day staring up at the ceiling, when I at least could have been sitting up and checking out what was going on" (Sienkiewicz - Mercer, 1989:94).

Ruth was severely disabled and could not move herself, and due to others decisions, she became restricted to spending most of her days in bed and her visual stimulation became less until other humane staff arrived on duty and placed her in a sitting position.

The disabled society just like the non-disabled society also have restrictions on their lives. Rules, regulations, laws and limits are all built within the societal system to maintain order and discipline.

Individuals have to live by these rules in order to be recognised as disabled. However they want just what everybody else has now, yet it is still being denied to them politically.

"Positivness is needed from artistic categories which constitute the parameters of his consciousness."
 (Giddens 1971:41).

Although Marx was using this idea in many areas which reflected life, his main feel was to divide or share each others thought equally.

Janet Holland, (1989) talks on why we need interaction and so does Mike Oliver. He says "To have the necessities to sustain life physically and make social relationships, hence being uninvolved with say preparations for the Christmas party or whatever special occasion which may arise, festivals and celebrations should include all citizens."

Oliver's statement could be said to be true in many ways as relationships are formed in the workplace or on the journey to work. There are however many people who are unemployed and do other things to contribute to their lifestyles such as charitable work i.e., working in youth clubs, helping out in children's play schemes during the school holidays, volunteers are always needed.

However, access is not always easy to buildings so already a barrier is in the individuals' way. The Committee On Restrictions Against Disabled People (CORAD) issued a report in 1982 to highlight problems that this present society causes.

It "stated that many people with impairments perceive access difficulties the most fundamental cause of discrimination" (Barnes 1990:158). Being unable to access most public and leisure facilities warrants a very silent and still life.

Abberley's contribution in Bartons Disability & Society (1996), quotes Gorz and says that "the abolition of work does not mean abolition of the need for effort, the desire for activity, the pleasure of creation, the need to cooperate with others and be of some use to the community. The demand to 'work less' does not mean or imply the right to 'rest more'." (Gorz 1982:2-3 ; Barton 1996:70)

As we have seen autonomy needs to be supported by others around us to enable an individual reach a specific goal, or as Rojak says "the freedom and choice what we have is obviously contingent upon place, time and above all, the actions of others" (Rojek 1995:1)

The disabled have been given laws in their own right, new points of view may help the disabled person integrate more easily into society and become as autonomous as possible i.e., due to the severity of disability.

Autonomy will then be viewed as a person having mental capacities to make choices "As we have seen, individuals express their autonomy with reference to their capacity to formulate consistent aims and strategies which they believe to be in their interests and their attempts to put them into practice in the activities in which they engage... Three key variables affect levels of individual autonomy: the level of understanding a person has about herself, her culture and what is expected of her... the psychological capacity she has to formulate options... and the objective opportunities enabling her to act accordingly (Faden & Beauchamp, 1986:241-56).

Research Method

The research method used was ethnographic, and a brief description will be given so we can see how the project was formulated.

"The relationship between ethnography and the people studied has been attacked as exploitative "(Hammersley, 1990).

This has been said by researchers for many reasons one of the main ones being that as the research is usually carried out in peoples natural surroundings people are more relaxed and therefore may be inclined to talk more about a situation, and as the researcher may not have debriefed the subject with all the information as to why they need to obtain this information a false light may have been put on the situation. Self-disclosure which Sabini describes as including "experiences, desires, fears fantasies, and so on" (Sabini,1992) of one's self is needed in-order for research to be conducted. However having said this, I did not use this method under false pretences as being a carer myself for ten years to my son, I have experienced many difficulties physically and emotionally. Using ethnographic research was the best way to collect qualitative data of this kind as using only questionnaires would not tell me about WU's lifestyles and autonomy, but only what percentage of WU's did certain activities hence missing the whole point of my research.

Scripts from other writers interviews previously mentioned will also be used in conjunction with my interviews as an attempt can then be made to analyse lives and head for any improvements that need to be discussed enabling able-bodied and others to understand how it is to be a WU in 1997.

Questionnaire

My questionnaire consisted of eleven guiding questions, which were used during the informal interviews. They were all used in the same order although other subjects were talked of due the nature of peoples experiences.

As it would not benefit myself or the interviewees to give yes no answers and explanations, a story of their lives will be told which will include the questions to give an all round insight to how a WU's life can be.

To gain a picture of cognitive depravation such as seen by Doyal and Goughs theory the following questions used were:

1) Did you go to a special or mainstream school and how did this prepare you for later life?

1A) What caused you to use a wheelchair?

2) Do you work?, If not would you like to?

3) Are social services or other government bodies in the day to day running of life?

4) If so are they doing what you would like them to do for you?

5) New disability laws are now being introduced by the government i.e., the Disability Discrimination Act which

came into force in 1996. What changes do you think they will make to your life?

The rest of the questions related to Restricted Opportunities, which as you have previously read about do not enable WU's and the disabled to live as full a life as could be possible.

6) Are there leisure places i.e., pubs, clubs, cinemas etc. that you feel restricted from?

7) Do you find people overfriendly and offering help when not needed? If so how do you deal with this?

8) Do you drive or have access to a car when needed?

9) Are you in a relationship right now? If not would you like to be?

10) Is your partner a wheelchair user?

11) Are many of your friends' wheelchair users?

12) When there are changes in benefits, independent living recommendations, mobility transport or anything else that may be of interest to you as a WU, do you have a social worker to inform you of changes or is information passed through the grapevine?

13) Would you like a social worker?

14) Is there anything else you would like to talk about or ask me about?

Although many of the questions asked were spoken of in great detail with my 3 interviewees', there is insufficient space to project all of their thoughts and answers.

I have therefore included what was important to me at the time. Hoping this work opens many peoples' minds towards how we can all live cohesively in the future.

Interviews

Interview 1
Name: Barney Chalk
Age: 29

Barney comes to Lympe Farm twice a week on Wednesdays and Saturdays to exercise with weights etc. His muscular physic and good looks is something which grabbed my attention as soon as I walked in the gym.

During our conversation I found out that he was formally Ronnie Scotts personal bouncer in his club and worked there for many years. His Drs think a virus called Travermylitis (which affects the spinal area), made Barney paralysed from the chest down and this put an end to this bouncers lifestyle but not to his thirst for life.

> Barney says he is happily divorced due to his viral problems amongst other things and enjoys being single, when asked about his relationship status he said

"I'm sort of in a relationship"

"Sort of, sort of" I replied", then we both laughed, I knew what he meant, with both of us exchanging information about relationships we wondered when do they become stable and if so why aren't we any good at this.

"How or does being a wheelchair user affect your personal life" I asked,

"Well I still pull my fair share of birds" he replied, well that's one way of putting it I thought.

During my conversation with Barney we got onto the subject of presentation of self. He thought first impressions, was a main vein to be looked at when people talk of disability. He said "People always appeared to view the disabled or wheelchair users as reliant, dependant and sitting in a corner dribbling and kept away from everyone instead of joining in with the mainstream flow of life." I replied that "not all disabled persons are as able-bodied as you, and as a carer my son is severely disabled, a quadriplegic. This means he has no ability to move his limbs in co-ordination.

There needs to be creative activities for wheelchair users and the disabled. Jenny Morris states how these personal symbols may be interpreted by others. "One of the biggest proofs assumed that, for me, sex was a thing of the past. I think this is a view shared by the majority. It may have little reality, yet I'm in an awful NHS wheelchair" he said.

When asked about restrictions of wheelchair use in the leisure area, he said planning in advance was the best move as people don't always think about narrow doorways and steps when inviting him to parties' etc.

Shopping also appeared to be no problem as he uses Medway Savercentre and everything is under one roof.

"Have you heard about the new disability discrimination act and what changes do you think may happen because of this" I asked.

He replied "Well I'm not very political, but I do keep in touch with what's happening, I watch From the Edge which is shown on Tuesdays BBC2 and that's about it."

Barney says he does not consider himself as disabled and he has mainly able-bodied friends, he lives independently and his only help from social services is having a woman come in and iron his clothes, this is not because he can't manage but he says he can't iron. How very male I said.

Barney does however drive a converted motability car and loves the freedom it brings; he does not work and does not want to work right now.

We rounded off the interview talking about transport and travel. Trips to Budapest, Russia or any eastern block country he said were hard and these countries were totally unprepared for the disabled as steps and narrow doorways were everywhere. Denmark however was the total opposite with ramped buses, dropped curves and people who didn't stare but said hello. He thinks London transport would not need to do a lot to change and there are lots of disabled people around.

A figure of 400,00 in Britain alone according to Mike Olivers 1996 lectures, access restrictions is seen as one of the major problems in life as stated earlier.

I found Barney to be very positive about himself and life, he is what I call an able-bodied disabled and this is the image he portrays well.

Interview 2
Name: Tracey Bishop
Aged: 27

"Hi, nice to meet you at last" were both our opening lines, this was because with three failed interview dates (twice on her part and once on mine) we had finally joined together. As Tracey's main reason for cancelling was work we started off on this note.

"So where do you work and what kind of thing do you do?" I asked.

"I'm a graduate trainee at BOC in the I.T. (Information Technology) department" she said "this consists of some travelling to different locations and teaching others what information technology is about.

Tracey has gained two degrees since becoming wheelchair bound.. Mental physicality will not be used within these works as all three interviewees were competent.

Cognitive depravation will therefore be counterproductive

We started the interview and Tracey informed me of her life at the point of where her life will become changed for good. The use of her legs had been taken away. How did she cope as a young woman who had not long exited out of puberty?

"Well, many of my friends came regularly to visit me in hospital, and when I returned to school some people ignored me whilst others came across and said hi." "Do you have any WU friends?" I asked. She replied "not really, I seem to have lost touch with friends made in the rehabilitation unit from hospital." "Hmmm, that's what happens sometimes."

I did not need to ask Tracey if she was in a relationship as my meeting with her was initially set up by her boyfriend Paul who was in my class at Uni, she did however go on to describe her relationship and said "I met Paul through my brother who attends you Uni and we have been going out together for two and a half years and now live with each other. We hope to get married soon and have children"

"O.K, so your injuries did not affect your childbearing abilities?" I asked rather shyly as flashbacks of Tom Shakespheres' interview on WUs' sexuality in which it states something to the effect of "Oh I didn't think you could be sexually active" came back.

Tracey was not shy in coming forward when giving me some lessons concerning anatomy, she said "Since I only had a partial spinal break, the sex education talks taught in hospital showed that me I could still child bear."

We then moved the topic onto the leisure area and I asked Tracey "So, what kind of things do you do in your leisure time?" She replied "We go to pubs a lot, and though steps can be a problem I can walk a few steps with assistance if necessary, but mainly we go to places with few steps or lifts"

"How do you feel in crowds, and does the height difference between you and them bear any significance?" I enquired.

"Well in a pub most of my friends sit down round a table and conversation is usually the main attraction, I did feel nervous in crowds at first and it took me four years to venture out alone after the accident" she said.

"That must have been very stressful for you as four years is a long time to stay in" I said

"It was hard but there was always someone to come with me if I felt like going out and now I'm fine" was her answer.

"Good" I replied. I then went on to ask about any hobbies. Her response was "I did used to ride horses but I don't do that anymore."

Tracey comes from a family of two brothers and mum and dad. She told me that some problems arose during her hospital stay as her younger brother was entering the teenage years, whilst she and her parents were busy going up and down to the hospital.

Everyone involved was very supportive and they all get on well nowadays, she does think her parents were a bit overprotective as she was the only girl and very outgoing. I found Tracey to be enthusiastic and hard working, being a WU has made some obvious differences to her life such as not wanting to continue horse riding which was a hobby she

136

previously had and enjoyed immensely, "I'd like to remember it as it was" she states.

Attending football matches to support Liverpool is something both her and Paul do when they have time and her sporty wheelchair fits in well. Tracey like Barney Chalk (previously interviewed) bought her own wheelchair and feels the NHS could offer more designs and give people a right to choose which is best for them as not everyone is the same.

If we return to the area of work in this conclusion, Mike Oliver's view shows its importance as an influential contributor to lifestyle. "Certain types of social relations are created" (Oliver 1993)

So even if Tracey does not go out for Friday afternoon pub sessions with work colleagues or attend any functions connected to the workforce, she knows these kinds of habits exist and the option is there if she decides to take it. Knowing how the different relationships and systems connected to a work environment function makes her position as a WU an active citizen and not a passive receiver.

Interview 3
Name: Patrick Bremner
Age: 55

Patrick was the first person I originally interviewed, but I decided to write this interview last, there is no particular reason as to why but he did portray a calmness not found in the other interviewees and this makes his interview easier to tackle, this may be due to his maturity. Being very nervous about interviewing I found Patrick was very understanding if and when I phrased the questions rather bluntly.

Doing ethnographic research causes a trading of information as people often investigate causes closely associated to themselves and Gilbert rightly states that "Numerous projects have been born out of personal history or experiences of the researcher" (Gilbert,1993:173).

So although I am not a WU myself, being a carer for a WU is associated with similar outlooks within certain areas of life.

Before Patrick became a WU he was a stock broker in the city and walked at least seven miles a day as his job consisted of him meeting investors etc of many different companies and offering his services as a Lloyds' broker.

In 1988 he was diagnosed as having Multiple Sclerosis which is a disease that breaks down your nervous system hence making parts of your body non functional.

"There are many things that frustrate me about this society and wheelchair users, there are so many restrictions" he replied and some of these will come up later during the interview. As I was still very nervous I rushed onto the next question which was about what changes do you think the new disability law will bring to you and others? "Not an ounce of difference" he replied

This I thought was unfair as new laws and ideas always take a while to find their place within society, being a Black British you still sometimes get treated as a foreigner because many people don't think you are a true British. I am one of many people who is happy that the race relations law was introduced in 1965.

"Maybe in a few years we will see a difference" I said

"Maybe, but a lot of employers etc. can't afford to change access to buildings etc, and London Transport would find it hard to ramp buses and trains, I mean they can't even afford to change the old carriages they have now and they need to find an excess of up to 2 billion pounds" he expressed. "Were do you think they will find or raise this money" I continued "Well were could they get it from unless the government raised taxes and London Underground would have to raise fares and this would put the public off from using this system at a time when we are trying to reduce car usage"

I had to agree with Patrick on this point as the transport system does need to become more convenient to attract more customers.

"So you don't think the laws have any use" I said

"Well, on the other hand all new buildings have to take disability into account which is a good thing
"But there are so many buildings already" I interrupted

"Exactly, exactly, I mean I find shopping a hassle as I can't get into a majority of shops so I need to ask a customer to get the shop assistant or call them myself and tell them what I need" he said.
This situation reminded me of the dependency theories such as Oliver's were he says that a persons' disability is seen by society as his/her own problem and not the problem of society's structure.

The medical model described earlier also reinforces the problem by constantly trying to change the person and not the environment, another example that springs to mind is the dependency felt by Ruth Sienkiewicz-Mercer who could not speak and state what position she would like to be placed in i.e., only being sat from out of her bed up to see what was happening around her when humane staff came on duty.

The frustration of living by someone else's' rules when you have some of your own to live out, totally disregards the human within a disabled body.

The conversation between Patrick and me turned around at this point as I disclosed my own problems faced with my son Ben and accessibility.

I told him of a trip to the Cinema in which we as a family wanted to sit at the front. I therefore pushed Ben to the front where my other children had sat down. Carefully placing the wheelchair out of harms' way, I proceeded to sit down and placed Ben in a seat. An usher came forward and said all wheelchair users must be sat at the back of the Cinema in the designated disabled place. I explained we had come as a family and wanted to be seated together. After much fuss, the Usher placed Bens' large pushchair to the back of the room in the wheelchair space.

"That's disgraceful treatment" Patrick replied and this pushed us into the area of leisure.

"I go to the Festival Hall on the Southbank and they do shows and theatrical productions, the carer is admitted free of charge and the disabled person pays a discount rate to enter, parking facilities are also good and excess staff are at hand to help" he said

"Brilliant" I replied then continued "We need more examples like this." Patrick agreed. Personal lives and problems felt was our next area of discussion.

Patrick said there was some conflict felt between his wife and himself. Most of the arguments caused because he feels she does not understand his problems though she has read up on

MS, he says "I best explain my position as having two weights on my feet and walking through treacle, I think she is also disappointed because my MS was discovered at a time when we should be doing things together now that the children have grown up"

"Mmm I do sympathise but do you have any home help from social services?"

"Yes, but it's not the same one all the time, they send regular ones on different days"

"How do you find the service" I said "Very good, they are caring, understanding and they listen to what I have to say, I find them to be diligent and they ask me what I want." "O.K., so they give you as much time as you want?"

"Whatever they can afford" he said "Yes it's all about money" I interrupted "things would be better if they did provide my electric wheelchair" he finished.

We then talked about politics and how he thought the Conservatives were very business minded whilst Labour worked on emotions, he informed me that Michael Howard was the MP for his area.

When asked if he would like to work again he said "I would love to work again" but he could not do his type of work because of the long distances he had to travel. I suggested the use of an electric wheelchair will more easily put him into society and become as autonomous as possible i.e., due to the severity of disability.

Autonomy will then be based on peoples' capacity to formulate consistent aims and strategies which they believe to be in their interests.
Their attempts to form integrations of mainstream and special schools may be an area to be expanded upon in the future.

"The integration of schools is a good idea but it depends on the severity of the individual" he said "More distress could be caused to the child and special education can help children blossom if input is given by the right teachers. You must remember that the wheelchair is lower than everyone else and the teacher could look right over the child's head making them feel intimidated."

Patrick went on to say that he knows what being ignored felt like as many people talk to his wife and ask her "does he take sugar" a line made famous by the radio programme of the same name. We finished off the interview by discussing if Patrick had any WU friends, but like the others not really and only at the gym, he did however belong to the WUs' Association who distribute newsletters containing information on relevant matters concerning the disabled.

We all know there are variations to disability, and with that brings the individuals view on how life becomes lived and projected. Giddens says "categories which constitute the parameters of his consciousness." (Giddens,1971:41).

Hence awareness of oneself and the drive pushing quality of life needs to be kept in mind

Afterthoughts in 2009

Doing this research gave me food for thought, I did not think I would find such positive views on life as most of the work I had read talks of misery and struggles, not to say that none of these exist but able-bodied people experience such feelings also, we do not live in a perfect world.

As said earlier a persons' autonomy does depend on how a persons' societal structure is formulated i.e., how much assistance is around to promote their chosen lifestyle and this society needs to do more in the way of making everyday life fairer for all.

If someone owns a shop which cannot facilitate wheelchairs then they should have a bell or alarm that attracts the shopkeeper to note a person may be having difficulty getting what they want, Sainsbury's' is one such shop that has realised this and have installed push button alarms in their petrol stations.

The lives of wheelchair users I interviewed were not as different as I thought they would be. However there were conflicting views on lifestyles, Patrick felt very dependent on people to help whilst Barney felt the opposite. Tracey did not mind help, and though this information was not included in her interview she told me that sometimes people are over helpful. She did not mind this as it can sometimes break the ice with able-bodied people and show them that she is ordinary.

My son Ben talked of in this piece of work sadly passed on to the ancestors in 1998. The other small children are now teenagers and will be on their way to making their own families in the not so distant future. Life indeed does go on and time it is the only healer for many ailments.

A time to reflect, strive and fulfil our lives, to head for the best that we can be. Time has truly shown me that irrespective of whom we are, everyone has a gift.

Many lessons have come into my life since 1997, some which have seemed rather harsh and painful, yet I have emerged out from the other end of the tunnel to become a much deeper thinker and humanitarian at large. I have also used my gift of writing to promote such works as these and other worthy causes.

I feel further possible research could be done on lives viewed by people who have been institutionalised whether it is mentally or physically as displayed in the last essay. Hopefully technology will increase and give people with disabilities the option to live independently or provide more support for others who have already started to live so. Its' great to see wheelchairs and buggies being driven onto buses which have been built and equipped to take these items. I have witnessed many disabled become able bodied due to a change of thought and design to London's Transport system.

However, there is much still to do to enable vast numbers of people local and nationwide, even worldwide to become integrative parts of the society they inhabit.

My thanks go to all who helped me to produce this piece of work. May we all be prepared to help each other on our journey's path, yet always re-member "You are the one that you have been waiting for"

This simply means, you may be the specialist you crave to see, or the inventor who has not yet been recognised.

In life we must tap into our gifts and use our potential for self and others.

AMENRAA

Bibliography

Barnes, C (1990). Cabbage Syndrome. The social construction of dependence. The Falmer pg158

Barton Disability & Society 1996

Doyle & Gough pg 182

Durkheim, Ed. Thompson & Tunstall:pg111

Faden & Beauchamp, 1986:pg241-56

Gilbert,1993:pg173

Giddens 1971

Griffiths, 1988; Parker 1994 pg251

Hammersley, 1990

Hayles 1996

Hugman (1991

Len Doyal and Ian Gough: A Theory of Human Need (1991

An analysis of Marx, Durkheim and Max Weber. Cambridge University press. London. pg 41

Morris 1996: pg75

Oliver M (1996) Oral lecture given at Greenwich University

Parker G. (1994) A four-way stretch? The politics of disability and caring in Disabling Barriers - Enabling Environments Eds. Swain J., Finklestein V., French S and Oliver M. Sage Publications, London:251.

Rojek, C. (1995) Decentring Leisure. Rethinking Leisure Theory. Sage Publications. London:6.

Sabini John, (1992), Social Psychology, W.W. Norton and Co. Ltd. London. pg 555.

Sienkiewicz - Mercer R, I Raise My Eyes To Say Yes, Grafton Books, London.

Swannell, J.(1986), (Ed). The Little Oxford Dictionary of Current English. Sixth Edition. Clarendon Press. Oxford.:86.

The Committee On Restrictions Against Disabled People (CORAD) report 1982

Welch C, (1996) Key issues in support in Gerald Hales (ed) Beyond Disability: Towards an Enabling Society, SAGE Publications, London:21.

Endword

I hope my writings have provided some vision and perspective on how we can learn to better express ourselves. Many of these essays were written when I was under immense pressure in my personal life, yet I still completed what I had set out to do, which was to finish the course. Knowing within myself that I can achieve anything I put my time, energy and will towards has helped me to keep a positive outlook on life, no matter what may be happening on the peripheries.

Within my bibliographies I have included certain writers and purposely left out book titles, so that this may encourage you to delve further into your own understanding.

As you will have seen, some of the marks awarded were poor to medium, yet, even with these I feel that some guidance, through a good reflection on where and why marks were lost, is better than none. Elaborating on the processes of my own understanding/over standing, assisted me to go on to do further higher education in the form of a Masters degree in Applied Psychoanalytic Theory.
I have found that it's best to work in an area one enjoys. Then, work and leisure can become unified.

I am now an independent Life Advisor, who writes health plans for public health agencies, attends public speaking events promoting my theories, and runs health workshops for the public.

Hopefully there are many students reading my work who will go on to surpass my mark of a 2.2, and you may be one of them. Gaining good marks helps produce confidence and a willingness to keep learning. Many people are of the notion that we stop learning when we reach adulthood. This idea is incorrect. Continuing to learn is a lifelong process, literally *from the cradle to the grave*. Embrace it.

"A mind is a terrible thing to waste." Martin Luther King.

On a personal note, I feel that life is more about participation than winning as we all have a 'winning' gift though some gifts may appear more obvious than others. This however, does not mean your gift is unworthy, all gifts need sharpening and nurturing. Hold no fears as these will only hinder you and resolve little in any situation you may face.

There are many books mentioned within my essays, recommended as further reading in these fields or use material from your tutor's reading lists.

Speaking with others on your course can also be a good helping hand. Learning from each other is something we do daily. Pursue this as a conscious option. Humility and acceptance of assistance may be seen by some as a weakness, yet always remember it is better for us all to *grow bright and right rather than wrong and strong.*

Wishing you much peace, love, and joy on your life's journey.

Hellen Adom

Lightning Source UK Ltd.
Milton Keynes UK
03 March 2011
168617UK00001B/1/P